The Constitution of
The State of Arizona
A Quick Reference Guide

Bootblack Budget Books
Copyright 2018 ©
ISBN-13: 978-1985343702
ISBN-10: 1985343703

Contents:

Preamble – Page 25

Article I: State Boundaries – Page 26

Section 1. Designation of boundaries

Section 2. Alteration of state boundaries

Article II: Declaration of Rights – Page 28

Section 1. Fundamental principles; recurrence to

Section 2. Political power; purpose of government

Section 3. Supreme law of the land

Section 4. Due process of law

Section 5. Right of petition and of assembly

Section 6. Freedom of speech and press

Section 7. Oaths and affirmations

Section 8. Right to privacy

Section 9. Irrevocable grants of privileges, franchises or immunities

Section 10. Self-incrimination; double jeopardy

Section 11. Administration of justice

Section 12. Liberty of conscience; appropriations for religious purposes prohibited; religious freedom

Section 13. Equal privileges and immunities

Section 14. Habeas corpus

Section 15. Excessive bail; cruel and unusual punishment

Section 16. Corruption of blood; forfeiture of estate

Section 17. Eminent domain; just compensation for private property taken; public use as judicial question

Section 18. Imprisonment for debt

Section 19. Bribery or illegal rebating; witnesses; self-incrimination no defense

Section 20. Military power subordinate to civil power

Section 21. Free and equal elections

Section 22. Bailable offenses

Section 23. Trial by jury; number of jurors specified by law

Section 24. Rights of accused in criminal prosecutions

Section 25. Bills of attainder; ex post facto laws; impairment of contract obligations

Section 26. Bearing arms

Section 27. Standing army; quartering soldiers

Section 28. Treason

Section 29. Hereditary emoluments, privileges or powers; perpetuities or entailments

Section 30. Indictment or information; preliminary examination

Section 31. Damages for death or personal injuries

Section 32. Constitutional provisions mandatory

Section 33. Reservation of rights

Section 34. Industrial pursuits by state and municipal corporations

Section 2.1. Victim's Bill of Rights

Article III: Distribution of Powers – Page 40

Section 1. Distribution of Powers

Article IV: Legislative Department – Page 41

Part I: Legislative Authority; Initiative and Referendum

Section 1. Legislative authority; initiative and referendum

Section 2. Penalty for violation of initiative and referendum provisions

Part II: The Legislature:

Section 1. Senate; house of representatives; members; special session upon petition of members; congressional and legislative boundaries; citizen commissions

Section 2. Qualifications of Members of Legislature

Section 3. Sessions of Legislature; Special Sessions; Limitation of Subjects for Consideration

Section 4. Disqualification for Membership in Legislature

Section 5. Ineligibility of Members of Legislature to Other Public Offices

Section 6. Privilege from Arrest; Civil Process

Section 7. Freedom of Debate

Section 8. Organization; Officers; Rules of Procedure

Section 9. Quorum; Compelling Attendance; Adjournment

Section 10. Journal of Proceedings; Roll Call

Section 11. Disorderly Behavior; Expulsion of Members

Section 12. Procedure on Bills; Approval or Disapproval by Governor

Section 13. Subject and Title of Bills

Section 14. Legislation by Reference Prohibited

Section 15. Passage of Bills by Majority; Signing of Bills

Section 16. Right to Protest

Section 17. Extra Compensation Prohibited; Increase or Decrease of Compensation During Term of Office

Section 18. Suits Against State

Section 19. Local or Special Laws

Section 20. Appropriation Bills

Section 21. Term Limits of Members of State Legislature

Section 22. Juvenile Justice; Certain Chronic and Violent Juvenile Offenders Prosecuted as Adults; Community Alternatives for Certain Juvenile Offenders; Public Proceedings and Records

Section 23. Passes and Purchase of Transportation by Public Officers; Inapplication to National Guard

Section 24. Enacting Clause of Bills; Initiative Bills

Section 25. Continuity of Governmental Operations in Emergency

Article V: Executive Department – Page 62

Section 1. Executive department; state officers; terms; election; residence and office at seat of government; duties

Section 2. Eligibility to state offices

Section 3. Governor, commander-in-chief of the military forces

Section 4. Governor; powers and duties; special sessions of legislature; message and recommendations

Section 5. Reprieves, commutations and pardons

Section 6. Death, resignation, removal or disability of governor; succession to office; impeachment, absence from state or temporary disability

Section 7. Presentation of bills to governor; approval; veto; filing with secretary of state; veto of items in appropriation bills; inapplication of veto power to referred bills

Section 8. Vacancies in office

Section 9. Powers and duties of state officers

Section 10. Canvass of election returns for state officers; certificates of election

Section 11. Commissions

Section 12. Compensation of elective state officers; commission on salaries for elective state officers

Article VI: Judicial Department – Page 69

Section 1. Judicial power; courts

Section 2. Supreme court; composition; divisions; decisions, transaction of business

Section 3. Supreme court; administrative supervision; chief justice

Section 4. Supreme court; term of office

Section 5. Supreme court; jurisdiction; writs; rules; habeas corpus

Section 6. Supreme court; qualifications of justices

Section 7. Supreme court; clerk and assistants; administrative director and staff

Section 8. Supreme court; publication of opinions

Section 9. Intermediate appellate courts

Section 10. Superior court; number of judges

Section 11. Superior court; presiding judges; duties

Section 12. Superior court; term of office

Section 13. Superior court; composition; salaries; judgments and proceedings; process

Section 14. Superior court; original jurisdiction

Section 15. Jurisdiction and authority in juvenile proceedings

Section 16. Superior court; appellate jurisdiction

Section 17. Superior court; conduct of business; trial juries; jury trial; grand juries

Section 18. Superior court; writs

Section 19. Superior court; service of judge in another county

Section 20. Retirement and service of retired justices and judges

Section 21. Superior court; speedy decisions

Section 22. Superior and other courts; qualifications of judges

Section 23. Superior court; clerk

Section 24. Superior court; court commissioners, masters and referees

Section 25. Style of process; conduct of prosecutions in name of state

Section 26. Oath of office

Section 27. Charge to juries; reversal of causes for technical error

Section 28. Justices and judges; dual office holding; political activity; practice of law

Section 30. Courts of record

Section 31. Judges pro tempore

Section 32. Justices of the peace and inferior courts; jurisdiction, powers and duties; terms of office; salaries

Section 33. Change by legislature in number of justices or judges; reduction of salary during term of office

Section 34. Absence of judicial officer from state

Section 35. Continuance in office; continued existence of offices; application of prior statute and rules

Section 36. Commission on appellate court appointments and terms, appointments and vacancies on commission

Section 37. Judicial vacancies and appointments; initial terms; residence; age

Section 38. Declaration of candidacy; form of judicial ballot, rejection and retention; failure to file declaration

Section 39. Retirement of justices and judges; vacancies

Section 40. Option for counties with less than two hundred fifty thousand persons

Section 41. Superior court divisions; commission on trial court appointments; membership; terms

Section 42. Retention evaluation of justices and judges

Article 6.1: Commission on Judicial Conduct – Page 93

Section 1. Composition; appointment; term; vacancies

Section 2. Disqualification of judge

Section 3. Suspension or removal of judge

Section 4. Retirement of judge

Section 5. Definitions and rules implementing article

Section 6. Article self-executing

Article VII : Suffrage and Elections – Page 96

Section 1. Method of voting; secrecy

Section 2. Qualifications of voters; disqualification

Section 3. Voting residence of federal employees and certain others

Section 4. Privilege of electors from arrest

Section 5. Military duty on day of election

Section 6. Residence of military personnel stationed within state

Section 7. Highest number of votes received as determinative of person elected

Section 8. Qualifications for voters at school elections

Section 9. Advisory vote

Section 10. Direct primary election law

Section 11. General elections; date

Section 12. Registration and other laws

Section 13. Submission of questions upon bond issues or special assessments

Section 14. Fee for placing candidate's name on ballot

Section 15. Qualifications for public office

Section 16. Campaign contributions and expenditures; publicity

Section 17. Vacancy in Congress

Section 18. Term limits on ballot appearances in congressional elections.

Article VIII: Removal from Office – Page 101

Part 1: Recall of Public Officers

Section 1. Officers subject to recall; petitioners

Section 2. Recall petitions; contents; filing; signatures; oath

Section 3. Resignation of officer; special election

Section 4. Special election; candidates; results; qualification of successor

Section 5. Recall petitions; restrictions and conditions

Section 6. Application of general election laws; implementary legislation

Part 2: Impeachments

Section 1. Power of impeachment in house of representatives; trial by senate

Section 2. Conviction; grounds for impeachment; judgment; liability to trial

Article IX: Public Debt, Revenue, and Taxation – Page 104

Section 1. Surrender of power of taxation; uniformity of taxes

Section 2. Property subject to taxation; exemptions

Section 2.1. Exemption from tax; property of widowers

Section 2.2. Exemption from tax; property of persons who are disabled

Section 2.3. Exemption from tax; increase in amount of exemptions, assessments and income

Section 3. Annual tax; purposes; amount; tax laws; payment of taxes into state treasury

Section 4. Fiscal year; annual statement of receipts and expenditures; deficit

Section 5. Power of state to contract debts; purposes; limit; restrictions

Section 6. Local assessments and taxes

Section 7. Gift or loan of credit; subsidies; stock ownership; joint ownership

Section 8. Local debt limits; assent of taxpayers

Section 8.1. Unified school district debt limit

Section 9. Statement of tax and objects

Section 10. Aid of church, private or sectarian school, or public service corporation

Section 11. Taxing procedure; license tax on registered vehicles

Section 12. Authority to provide for levy and collection of license and other taxes

Section 12.1. Temporary taxes; repeal from and after May 31, 2013

Section 13. Inventory, materials and products of manufacturers; production livestock and animals; tax exemption

Section 14. Use and distribution of vehicle, user, and gasoline and diesel tax receipts

Section 15. License tax on aircraft

Section 16. Exemption of watercraft from ad valorem property taxes

Section 17. Economic estimates commission; appropriation limitation; powers and duties of commission

Section 18. Residential ad valorem tax limits; limit on increase in values; definitions

Section 19. Limitation on annual increases in local ad valorem tax levies; exceptions

Section 20. Expenditure limitation; adjustments; reporting

Section 21. Expenditure limitations for school districts and community college districts

Section 22. Vote required to increase state revenues; application; exceptions

Section 23. Expenditures required by initiative or referendum; funding source

Section 24. Prohibition of new real property sale or transfer taxes

Article X: State and School Lands – Page 110

Section 1. Acceptance and holding of lands by state in trust

Section 2. Unauthorized disposition of land or proceeds as breach of trust

Section 3. Mortgage or other encumbrance; sale or lease at public auction

Section 4. Sale or other disposal; appraisal; minimum price; credit; passing of title

Section 5. Minimum price; relinquishment of lands to United States

Section 6. Lands reserved by United States for development of water power

Section 7. Establishment of permanent funds; segregation, investment and distribution of monies; exception; resolution of litigation

Section 8. Conformity of contracts with enabling act

Section 9. Sale or lease; conditions; limitations; lease prior to adoption of constitution

Section 10. Laws for sale or lease of state lands; protection of residents and lessees

Section 11. Maximum acreage allowed single purchaser

Section 12. Land exchanges; purposes; notice; hearings; submission to the voters

Article XI : Education – Page 121

Section 1. Public school system; education of pupils who are hearing and vision impaired

Section 2. Conduct and supervision of school system

Section 3. State board of education; composition; powers and duties; compensation

Section 4. State superintendent of public instruction; board membership; powers and duties

Section 5. Regents of university and other governing boards; appointments by governor; membership of governor on board of regents

Section 6. Admission of students of both sexes to state educational institutions; tuition; common school system

Section 7. Sectarian instruction; religious or political test or qualification

Section 8. Permanent state school fund; source; apportionment of state funds

Section 9. County school fund; size of fund; free schools

Section 10. Source of revenue for maintenance of state educational institutions

Section 11. Schools; inflation adjustments; exceptions; definitions

Article XII: Counties – Page 128

Section 1. Counties as bodies politic and corporate

Section 2. Counties of territory as counties of state

Section 3. County officers; election; term of office

Section 4. County officers; duties, powers, and qualifications; salaries

Section 5. Charter committee; charter preparation; approval

Section 6. Amendment of charter

Section 7. County charter provisions

Section 8. Government and other powers

Section 9. Self-executing provision

Article XIII: Municipal Corporations – Page 136

Section 1. Incorporation and organization; classification

Section 2. Charter; preparation and proposal by board of freeholders; ratification and approval; amendment

Section 3. Election of board of freeholders

Section 4. Franchises; approval of electors; term

Section 5. Right of municipal corporation to engage in business or enterprise

Section 6. Franchises; restrictions

Section 7. Irrigation and other districts as political subdivisions

Article XIV: Corporations other than Municipal – Page 140

Section 1. "Corporation" defined; right to sue and suability

Section 2. Formation under general laws; change of laws; regulation

Section 3. Existing charters

Section 4. Restriction to business authorized by charter or law

Section 5. Foreign corporations; transaction of business

Section 6. Stocks; bonds

Section 7. Lease or alienation of franchise

Section 8. Filing of articles of incorporation; place of business; agent for service of process; venue

Section 9. Eminent domain; taking corporate property and franchises for public use

Section 10. Elections for directors or managers

Section 11. Liability of stockholders

Section 12. Officers of banking institutions; individual responsibility

Section 13. Want of legal organization as a defense

Section 14. Legislative power to impose conditions

Section 15. Monopolies and trusts

Section 16. Records, books, and files; visitorial and inquisitorial powers of state

Section 17. Fees; reports; licensing of foreign corporations

Section 18. Contributions to influence elections or official action

Section 19. Penalties for violation of article

Article XV: The Corporation Commission – Page 146

Section 1. Term limits on corporation commission; composition; election; office vacancies; qualifications

Section 2. "Public service corporations" defined

Section 3. Power of commission as to classifications, rates and charges, rules, contracts, and accounts; local regulation

Section 4. Power to inspect and investigate

Section 5. Power to issue certificates of incorporation and licenses

Section 6. Enlargement of powers by legislature; rules and regulations

Section 7. Connecting and intersecting lines of transportation and communications corporations

Section 8. Transportation by connecting carriers

Section 9. Transmission of messages by connecting carriers

Section 10. Railways as public highways; other corporations as common carriers

Section 11. Movable property as personal property; liability of property to attachment, execution and sale

Section 12. Charges for service; discrimination; free or reduced rate transportation

Section 13. Reports to commission

Section 14. Value of property of public service corporations

Section 15. Acceptance of constitutional provisions by existing corporations

Section 16. Forfeitures for violations

Section 17. Appeal to courts

Section 19. Power to impose fines

Article XVI: Militia – Page 153

Section 1. Composition of militia

Section 2. Composition and designation of organized militia

Section 3. Conformity to federal regulations

Article XVII: Water Rights – Page 154

Section 1. Riparian water rights

Section 2. Recognition of existing rights

Article XVIII: Labor – Page 155

Section 1. Eight-hour day

Section 2. Child labor

Section 3. Contractual immunity of employer from liability for negligence

Section 4. Fellow servant doctrine

Section 5. Contributory negligence and assumption of risk

Section 6. Recovery of damages for injuries

Section 7. Employer's liability law

Section 8. Workmen's compensation law

Section 9. Blacklists

Section 10. Employment of aliens

Article XIX: Mines – Page 159

Section 1. Mines

Article XX: Ordinance – Page 160

Section 1. Toleration of religious sentiment

Section 2. Polygamy

Section 3. Introduction of intoxicating liquors into Indian country

Section 4. Public lands; Indian lands

Section 5. Taxation

Section 6. Territorial debts and liabilities

Section 7. Public school system; suffrage

Section 8. English language

Section 9. Location of state capital

Section 12. Lands granted to state

Section 13. Ordinance as part of constitution; amendment

Article XXI: Mode of Amending – Page 164

Section 1. Introduction in legislature; initiative petition; election

Section 2. Convention

Article XXII: Schedule and Miscellaneous – Page 166

Section 1. Existing rights, actions, suits, proceedings, contracts, claims, or demands; process

Section 2. Territorial laws

Section 3. Debts, fines, penalties, and forfeitures

Section 4. Recognizances; bonds; estate; judgments; choses in action

Section 5. Criminal prosecutions and penal actions; offenses; penalties; actions and suits

Section 6. Territorial, district, county, and precinct officers

Section 7. Causes pending in district courts of territory; records, papers, and property

Section 8. Probate records and proceedings

Section 9. Causes pending in supreme court of territory; records, papers, and property

Section 10. Seals of supreme court, superior courts, municipalities, and county officers

Section 11. Effective date of constitution

Section 12. Election of representative in congress

Section 13. Continuation in office until qualification of successor

Section 14. Initiative

Section 15. Public institutions

Section 16. Confinement of minor offenders

Section 17. Compensation of public officers

Section 18. Nomination of incumbent public officers to other offices

Section 19. Lobbying

Section 20. Design of state seal

Section 21. Enactment of laws to carry constitution into effect

Section 22. Judgments of death

Article XXV: Right to Work – Page 173

Section 1. Right to work or employment without membership in labor organization

Article XXXVI: Right of Licensed Real Estate Brokers and Salesmen to Prepare Instruments Incident to Property Transactions – Page 174

Section 1. Powers of real estate broker or salesman

Article XXVII: Regulation of Public Health, Safety and Welfare – Page 175

Section 1. Regulation of ambulances; powers of legislature

Section 2. Health care; definitions

Article XXVIII: English as the Official Language – Page 176

Section 1. Definitions

Section 2. Official language of Arizona

Section 3. Preserving and enhancing the role of the official

Section 4. Official actions to be conducted in English

Section 5. Rules of construction

Section 6. Standing; notification of attorney general; recovery of costs

Article XXIX : Public Retirement Systems – Page 180

Section 1. Public retirement systems

Article XXX: Marriage – Page 181

Section 1. Marriage

Preamble

We the people of the State of Arizona, grateful to Almighty God for our liberties, do ordain this Constitution.

Article I: State Boundaries

Section 1. Designation of Boundaries

The boundaries of the State of Arizona shall be as follows, namely: Beginning at a point on the Colorado River twenty English miles below the junction of the Gila and Colorado Rivers, as fixed by the Gadsden Treaty between the United States and Mexico, being in latitude thirty-two degrees, twenty-nine minutes, forty-four and forty-five one-hundredths seconds north and longitude one hundred fourteen degrees, forty-eight minutes, forty-four and fifty-three one -hundredths seconds west of Greenwich; thence along and with the international boundary line between the United States and Mexico in a southeastern direction to Monument Number 127 on said boundary line in latitude thirty-one degrees, twenty minutes north; thence east along and with said parallel of latitude, continuing on said boundary line to an intersection with the meridian of longitude one hundred nine degrees, two minutes, fifty-nine and twenty-five one-hundredths seconds west, being identical with the southwestern corner of New Mexico; thence north along and with said meridian of longitude and the west boundary of New Mexico to an intersection with the parallel of latitude thirty-seven degrees north, being the common corner of Colorado, Utah, Arizona, and New Mexico; thence west along and with said parallel of latitude and the south boundary of Utah to an intersection with the meridian of longitude one hundred fourteen degrees, two minutes, fifty-nine and twenty-five one-hundredths seconds west, being on the east boundary line of the State of Nevada; thence south along and with said meridian of longitude and the east boundary of said State of Nevada, to the center of the Colorado River; thence down the mid-channel of said Colorado River in a southern direction along and with the east boundaries of Nevada, California, and the Mexican Territory of Lower California, successively, to the place of beginning.

Section 2. Alteration of State Boundaries

The legislature, in cooperation with the properly constituted authority of any adjoining state, is empowered to change, alter, and redefine the state boundaries, such change, alteration and redefinition to become effective only upon approval of the Congress of the United States.

Article II: Declaration Of Rights

Section 1. Fundamental Principles; Recurrence To

A frequent recurrence to fundamental principles is essential to the security of individual rights and the perpetuity of free government.

Section 2. Political Power; Purpose of Government

All political power is inherent in the people, and governments derive their just powers from the consent of the governed, and are established to protect and maintain individual rights.

Section 2.1. Victims' bill of rights

(A): To preserve and protect victims' rights to justice and due process, a victim of crime has a right:

1. To be treated with fairness, respect, and dignity, and to be free from intimidation, harassment, or abuse, throughout the criminal justice process.

2. To be informed, upon request, when the accused or convicted person is released from custody or has escaped.

3. To be present at and, upon request, to be informed of all criminal proceedings where the defendant has the right to be present.

4. To be heard at any proceeding involving a post-arrest release decision, a negotiated plea, and sentencing.

5. To refuse an interview, deposition, or other discovery request by the defendant, the defendant's attorney, or other person acting on behalf of the defendant.

6. To confer with the prosecution, after the crime against the victim has been charged, before trial or before any disposition of the case and to be informed of the disposition.

7. To read pre-sentence reports relating to the crime against the victim when they are available to the defendant.

8. To receive prompt restitution from the person or persons convicted of the criminal conduct that caused the victim's loss or injury.

9. To be heard at any proceeding when any post-conviction release from confinement is being considered.

10. To a speedy trial or disposition and prompt and final conclusion of the case after the conviction and sentence.

11. To have all rules governing criminal procedure and the admissibility of evidence in all criminal proceedings protect victims' rights and to have these rules be subject to amendment or repeal by the legislature to ensure the protection of these rights.

12. To be informed of victims' constitutional rights.

(B) A victim's exercise of any right granted by this section shall not be grounds for dismissing any criminal proceeding or setting aside any conviction or sentence.

(C) "Victim" means a person against whom the criminal offense has been committed or, if the person is killed or incapacitated, the person's spouse, parent, child or other lawful representative, except if the person is in custody for an offense or is the accused.

(D) The legislature, or the people by initiative or referendum, have the authority to enact substantive and procedural laws to define, implement, preserve and protect the rights guaranteed to victims by this section, including the authority to extend any of these rights to juvenile proceedings.

(E) The enumeration in the constitution of certain rights for victims shall not be construed to deny or disparage others granted by the legislature or retained by victims.

Section 3. Supreme law of the land; authority to exercise sovereign authority against federal action; use of government personnel and financial resources

A. The Constitution of the United States is the supreme law of the land to which all government, state and federal, is subject.

B. To protect the people's freedom and to preserve the checks and balances of the United States Constitution, this state may exercise its sovereign authority to restrict the actions of its personnel and the use of its financial resources to purposes that are consistent with the constitution by doing any of the following:

1. Passing an initiative or referendum pursuant to article IV, part 1, section 1.

2. Passing a bill pursuant to article IV, part 2 and article V, section 7.

3. Pursuing any other available legal remedy.

C. If the people or their representatives exercise their authority pursuant to this section, this state and all political subdivisions of this state are prohibited from using any personnel or financial resources to enforce, administer or cooperate with the designated federal action or program.

Section 4. Due process of law

No person shall be deprived of life, liberty, or property without due process of law.

Section 5. Right of petition and of assembly

The right of petition, and of the people peaceably to assemble for the common good, shall never be abridged.

Section 6. Freedom of speech and press

Every person may freely speak, write, and publish on all subjects, being responsible for the abuse of that right.

Section 7. Oaths and affirmations

The mode of administering an oath, or affirmation, shall be such as shall be most consistent with and binding upon the conscience of the person to whom such oath, or affirmation, may be administered.

Section 8. Right to privacy

No person shall be disturbed in his private affairs, or his home invaded, without authority of law.

Section 9. Irrevocable grants of privileges, franchises or immunities

No law granting irrevocably any privilege, franchise, or immunity shall be enacted.

Section 10. Self-incrimination; double jeopardy

No person shall be compelled in any criminal case to give evidence against himself, or be twice put in jeopardy for the same offense.

Section 11. Administration of justice

Justice in all cases shall be administered openly, and without unnecessary delay.

Section 12. Liberty of conscience; appropriations for religious purposes prohibited; religious freedom

The liberty of conscience secured by the provisions of this constitution shall not be so construed as to excuse acts of licentiousness, or justify practices inconsistent with the peace and safety of the state. No public money or property shall be appropriated for or applied to any religious worship, exercise, or instruction, or to the support of any religious establishment. No religious qualification shall be required for any public office or employment, nor shall any person be incompetent as a witness or juror in consequence of his opinion on matters of religion, nor be questioned touching his religious belief in any court of justice to affect the weight of his testimony.

Section 13. Equal privileges and immunities

No law shall be enacted granting to any citizen, class of citizens, or corporation other than municipal, privileges or immunities which, upon the same terms, shall not equally belong to all citizens or corporations.

Section 14. Habeas corpus

The privilege of the writ of habeas corpus shall not be suspended by the authorities of the state.

Section 15. Excessive bail; cruel and unusual punishment

Excessive bail shall not be required, nor excessive fines imposed, nor cruel and unusual punishment inflicted.

Section 16. Corruption of blood; forfeiture of estate

No conviction shall work corruption of blood, or forfeiture of estate.

Section 17. Eminent domain; just compensation for private property taken; public use as judicial question

Private property shall not be taken for private use, except for private ways of necessity, and for drains, flumes, or ditches, on or across the lands of others for mining, agricultural, domestic, or sanitary purposes. No private property shall be taken or damaged for public or private use without just compensation having first been made, paid into court for the owner, secured by bond as may be fixed by the court, or paid into the state treasury for the owner on such terms and conditions as the legislature may provide, and no right of way shall be appropriated to the use of any corporation other than municipal, until full compensation therefor be first made in money, or ascertained and paid into court for the owner, irrespective of any benefit from any improvement proposed by such corporation, which compensation shall be ascertained by a jury, unless a jury be waived as in other civil cases in courts of record, in the manner prescribed by law. Whenever an attempt is made to take private property for a use alleged to be public, the question whether the contemplated use be really public shall be a judicial question, and determined as such without regard to any legislative assertion that the use is public.

Section 18. Imprisonment for debt

There shall be no imprisonment for debt, except in cases of fraud.

Section 19. Bribery or illegal rebating; witnesses; self-incrimination no defense

Any person having knowledge or possession of facts that tend to establish the guilt of any other person or corporation charged with bribery or illegal rebating, shall not be excused from giving testimony or producing evidence, when legally called upon to do so, on the ground that it may tend to incriminate him under the laws of the state; but no person shall be prosecuted or subject to any penalty or forfeiture for, or on account of, any transaction, matter, or thing concerning which he may so testify or produce evidence.

Section 20. Military power subordinate to civil power

The military shall be in strict subordination to the civil power.

Section 21. Free and equal elections

All elections shall be free and equal, and no power, civil or military, shall at any time interfere to prevent the free exercise of the right of suffrage.

Section 22. Bailable offenses

A. All persons charged with crime shall be bailable by sufficient sureties, except:

1. For capital offenses, sexual assault, sexual conduct with a minor under fifteen years of age or molestation of a child under fifteen years of age when the proof is evident or the presumption great.

2. For felony offenses committed when the person charged is already admitted to bail on a separate felony charge and where the proof is evident or the presumption great as to the present charge.

3. For felony offenses if the person charged poses a substantial danger to any other person or the community, if no conditions of release which may be imposed will reasonably assure the safety of the other person or the community and if the proof is evident or the presumption great as to the present charge.

4. For serious felony offenses as prescribed by the legislature if the person charged has entered or remained in the United States illegally and if the proof is evident or the presumption great as to the present charge.

B. The purposes of bail and any conditions of release that are set by a judicial officer include:

1. Assuring the appearance of the accused.

2. Protecting against the intimidation of witnesses.

3. Protecting the safety of the victim, any other person or the community.

Section 23. Trial by jury; number of jurors specified by law

The right of trial by jury shall remain inviolate. Juries in criminal cases in which a sentence of death or imprisonment for thirty years or more is authorized by law shall consist of twelve persons. In all criminal cases the unanimous consent of the jurors shall be necessary to render a verdict. In all other cases, the number of jurors, not less than six, and the number required to render a verdict, shall be specified by law.

Section 24. Rights of accused in criminal prosecutions

In criminal prosecutions, the accused shall have the right to appear and defend in person, and by counsel, to demand the nature and cause of the accusation against him, to have a copy thereof, to testify in his own behalf, to meet the witnesses against him face to face, to have compulsory process to compel the attendance of witnesses in his own behalf, to have a speedy public trial by an impartial jury of the county in which the offense is alleged to have been committed, and the right to appeal in all cases; and in no instance shall any accused person before final judgment be compelled to advance money or fees to secure the rights herein guaranteed.

Section 25. Bills of attainder; ex post facto laws; impairment of contract obligations

No bill of attainder, ex-post-facto law, or law impairing the obligation of a contract, shall ever be enacted.

Section 26. Bearing arms

The right of the individual citizen to bear arms in defense of himself or the state shall not be impaired, but nothing in this section shall be construed as authorizing individuals or corporations to organize, maintain, or employ an armed body of men.

Section 27. Standing army; quartering soldiers

No standing army shall be kept up by this state in time of peace, and no soldier shall in time of peace be quartered in any house without the consent of its owner, nor in time of war except in the manner prescribed by law.

Section 28. Treason

Treason against the state shall consist only in levying war against the state, or adhering to its enemies, or in giving them aid and comfort. No person shall be convicted of treason unless on the testimony of two witnesses to the same overt act, or confession in open court.

Section 29. Hereditary emoluments, privileges or powers; perpetuities or entailments

No hereditary emoluments, privileges, or powers shall be granted or conferred, and no law shall be enacted permitting any perpetuity or entailment in this state.

Section 30. Indictment or information; preliminary examination

No person shall be prosecuted criminally in any court of record for felony or misdemeanor, otherwise than by information or indictment; no person shall be prosecuted for felony by information without having had a preliminary examination before a magistrate or having waived such preliminary examination.

Section 31. Damages for death or personal injuries

No law shall be enacted in this state limiting the amount of damages to be recovered for causing the death or injury of any person, except that a crime victim is not subject to a claim for damages by a person who is harmed while the person is attempting to engage in, engaging in or fleeing after having engaged in or attempted to engage in conduct that is classified as a felony offense.

Section 32. Constitutional provisions mandatory

The provisions of this Constitution are mandatory, unless by express words they are declared to be otherwise.

Section 33. Reservation of rights

The enumeration in this Constitution of certain rights shall not be construed to deny others retained by the people.

Section 34. Industrial pursuits by state and municipal corporations

The state of Arizona and each municipal corporation within the state of Arizona shall have the right to engage in industrial pursuits.

Section 35. Actions by illegal aliens prohibited

A person who is present in this state in violation of federal immigration law related to improper entry by an alien shall not be awarded punitive damages in any action in any court in this state.

Section 36. Preferential treatment or discrimination prohibited; exceptions; definition

A. This state shall not grant preferential treatment to or discriminate against any individual or group on the basis of race, sex, color, ethnicity or national origin in the operation of public employment, public education or public contracting.

B. This section does not:

1. Prohibit bona fide qualifications based on sex that are reasonably necessary to the normal operation of public employment, public education or public contracting.

2. Prohibit action that must be taken to establish or maintain eligibility for any federal program, if ineligibility would result in a loss of federal monies to this state.

3. Invalidate any court order or consent decree that is in force as of the effective date of this section.

C. The remedies available for a violation of this section are the same, regardless of the injured party's race, sex, color, ethnicity or national origin, as are otherwise available for a violation of the existing antidiscrimination laws of this state.

D. This section applies only to actions that are taken after the effective date of this section.

E. This section is self-executing.

F. For the purposes of this section, "state" includes this state, a city, town or county, a public university, including the university of Arizona, Arizona state university and northern Arizona university, a community college district, a school district, a special district or any other political subdivision in this state.

Section 37. Right to secret ballot; employee representation

The right to vote by secret ballot for employee representation is fundamental and shall be guaranteed where local, state or federal law permits or requires elections, designations or authorizations for employee representation.

Article III: Distribution of Powers

DISTRIBUTION OF POWERS

The powers of the government of the state of Arizona shall be divided into three separate departments, the legislative, the executive, and the judicial; and, except as provided in this constitution, such departments shall be separate and distinct, and no one of such departments shall exercise the powers properly belonging to either of the others.

Article IV: Legislative Department

Part 1: Legislative authority; initiative and referendum

Section 1.

(1) Senate; house of representatives; reservation of power to people.

The legislative authority of the state shall be vested in the legislature, consisting of a senate and a house of representatives, but the people reserve the power to propose laws and amendments to the constitution and to enact or reject such laws and amendments at the polls, independently of the legislature; and they also reserve, for use at their own option, the power to approve or reject at the polls any act, or item, section, or part of any act, of the legislature.

(2) Initiative power.

The first of these reserved powers is the initiative. Under this power ten per centum of the qualified electors shall have the right to propose any measure, and fifteen per centum shall have the right to propose any amendment to the constitution.

(3) Referendum power; emergency measures; effective date of acts.

The second of these reserved powers is the referendum. Under this power the legislature, or five per centum of the qualified electors, may order the submission to the people at the polls of any measure, or item, section, or part of any measure, enacted by the legislature, except laws immediately necessary for the preservation of the public peace, health, or safety, or for the support and maintenance of the departments of the state government and state institutions; but to allow opportunity for referendum petitions, no act passed by the legislature shall be operative for ninety days after the close of the session of the legislature enacting such measure, except such as require earlier operation to preserve the public peace, health, or safety, or to provide appropriations for the support and maintenance of the departments of the state and of state institutions; provided, that no such emergency measure shall be considered passed by the legislature unless it shall state in a separate section why it is necessary that it shall become immediately operative, and shall be approved by the affirmative votes of two-thirds of the members elected to each house of the legislature, taken by roll call of ayes and nays, and also approved by the governor; and should such measure be vetoed by the governor, it shall not become a law unless it shall be approved by the votes of three-fourths of the members elected to each house of the legislature, taken by roll call of ayes and nays.

(4) Initiative and referendum petitions; filing.

All petitions submitted under the power of the initiative shall be known as initiative petitions, and shall be filed with the secretary of state not less than four months preceding the date of the election at which the measures so proposed are to be voted upon. All petitions submitted under the power of the referendum shall be known as referendum petitions, and shall be filed with the secretary of state not more than ninety days after the final adjournment of the session of the legislature which shall have passed the measure to which the referendum is applied. The filing of a referendum petition against any item, section, or part of any measure shall not prevent the remainder of such measure from becoming operative.

(5) Effective date of initiative and referendum measures.

Any measure or amendment to the constitution proposed under the initiative, and any measure to which the referendum is applied, shall be referred to a vote of the qualified electors, and shall become law when approved by a majority of the votes cast thereon and upon proclamation of the governor, and not otherwise.

(6) (A) Veto of initiative or referendum.

The veto power of the governor shall not extend to an initiative measure approved by a majority of the votes cast thereon or to a referendum measure decided by a majority of the votes cast thereon.

(B) Legislature's power to repeal initiative or referendum.

The legislature shall not have the power to repeal an initiative measure approved by a majority of the votes cast thereon or to repeal a referendum measure decided by a majority of the votes cast thereon.

(C) Legislature's power to amend initiative or referendum.

The legislature shall not have the power to amend an initiative measure approved by a majority of the votes cast thereon, or to amend a referendum measure decided by a majority of the votes cast thereon, unless the amending legislation furthers the purposes of such measure and at least three-fourths of the members of each house of the legislature, by a roll call of ayes and nays, vote to amend such measure.

(D) Legislature's power to appropriate or divert funds created by initiative or referendum.

The legislature shall not have the power to appropriate or divert funds created or allocated to a specific purpose by an initiative measure approved by a majority of the votes cast thereon, or by a referendum measure decided by a majority of the votes cast thereon, unless the appropriation or diversion of funds furthers the purposes of such measure and at least three-fourths of the members of each house of the legislature, by a roll call of ayes and nays, vote to appropriate or divert such funds.

(7) Number of qualified electors.

The whole number of votes cast for all candidates for governor at the general election last preceding the filing of any initiative or referendum petition on a state or county measure shall be the basis on which the number of qualified electors required to sign such petition shall be computed.

(8) Local, city, town or county matters.

The powers of the initiative and the referendum are hereby further reserved to the qualified electors of every incorporated city, town, and county as to all local, city, town, or county matters on which such incorporated cities, towns, and counties are or shall be empowered by general laws to legislate. Such incorporated cities, towns, and counties may prescribe the manner of exercising said powers within the restrictions of general laws. Under the power of the initiative fifteen per centum of the qualified electors may propose measures on such local, city, town, or county matters, and ten per centum of the electors may propose the referendum on legislation enacted within and by such city, town, or county. Until provided by general law, said cities and towns may prescribe the basis on which said percentages shall be computed.

(9) Form and contents of initiative and of referendum petitions; verification.

Every initiative or referendum petition shall be addressed to the secretary of state in the case of petitions for or on state measures, and to the clerk of the board of supervisors, city clerk, or corresponding officer in the case of petitions for or on county, city, or town measures; and shall contain the declaration of each petitioner, for himself, that he is a qualified elector of the state (and in the case of petitions for or on city, town, or county measures, of the city, town, or county affected), his post office address, the street and number, if any, of his residence, and the date on which he signed such petition. Each sheet containing petitioners' signatures shall be attached to a full and correct copy of the title and text of the measure so proposed to be initiated or referred to the people, and every sheet of every such petition containing signatures shall be verified by the affidavit of the person who circulated said sheet or petition, setting forth that each of the names on said sheet was signed in the presence of the affiant and that in the belief of the affiant each signer was a qualified elector of the state, or in the case of a city, town, or county measure, of the city, town, or county affected by the measure so proposed to be initiated or referred to the people.

(10) Official ballot.

When any initiative or referendum petition or any measure referred to the people by the legislature shall be filed, in accordance with this section, with the secretary of state, he shall cause to be printed on the official ballot at the next regular general election the title and number of said measure, together with the words "yes" and "no" in such manner that the electors may express at the polls their approval or disapproval of the measure.

(11) Publication of measures.

The text of all measures to be submitted shall be published as proposed amendments to the constitution are published, and in submitting such measures and proposed amendments the secretary of state and all other officers shall be guided by the general law until legislation shall be especially provided therefor.

(12) Conflicting measures or constitutional amendments.

If two or more conflicting measures or amendments to the constitution shall be approved by the people at the same election, the measure or amendment receiving the greatest number of affirmative votes shall prevail in all particulars as to which there is conflict.

(13) Canvass of votes; proclamation.

It shall be the duty of the secretary of state, in the presence of the governor and the chief justice of the supreme court, to canvass the votes for and against each such measure or proposed amendment to the constitution within thirty days after the election, and upon the completion of the canvass the governor shall forthwith issue a proclamation, giving the whole number of votes cast for and against each measure or proposed amendment, and declaring such measures or amendments as are approved by a majority of those voting thereon to be law.

(14) Reservation of legislative power.

This section shall not be construed to deprive the legislature of the right to enact any measure except that the legislature shall not have the power to adopt any measure that supersedes, in whole or in part, any initiative measure approved by a majority of the votes cast thereon or any referendum measure decided by a majority of the votes cast thereon unless the superseding measure furthers the purposes of the initiative or referendum measure and at least three-fourths of the members of each house of the legislature, by a roll call of ayes and nays, vote to supersede such initiative or referendum measure.

(15) Legislature's right to refer measure to the people.

Nothing in this section shall be construed to deprive or limit the legislature of the right to order the submission to the people at the polls of any measure, item, section, or part of any measure.

(16) Self-executing.

This section of the constitution shall be, in all respects, self-executing.

Section II. Penalty for violation of initiative and referendum provisions

(1) The legislature shall provide a penalty for any willful violation of any of the provisions of the preceding section.

Part 2. The Legislature

Section 1.

(1) Senate; house of representatives; members; special session upon petition of members; congressional and legislative boundaries; citizen commissions

The senate shall be composed of one member elected from each of the thirty legislative districts established pursuant to this section.

The house of representatives shall be composed of two members elected from each of the thirty legislative districts established pursuant to this section.

(2) Upon the presentation to the governor of a petition bearing the signatures of not less than two-thirds of the members of each house, requesting a special session of the legislature and designating the date of convening, the governor shall promptly call a special session to assemble on the date specified. At a special session so called the subjects which may be considered by the legislature shall not be limited.

(3) By February 28 of each year that ends in one, an independent redistricting commission shall be established to provide for the redistricting of congressional and state legislative districts. The independent redistricting commission shall consist of five members. No more than two members of the independent redistricting commission shall be members of the same political party. Of the first four members appointed, no more than two shall reside in the same county. Each member shall be a registered Arizona voter who has been continuously registered with the same political party or registered as unaffiliated with a political party for three or more years immediately preceding appointment, who is committed to applying the provisions of this section in an honest, independent and impartial fashion and to upholding public confidence in the integrity of the redistricting process. Within the three years previous to appointment, members shall not have been appointed to, elected to, or a candidate for any other public office, including precinct committeeman or committeewoman but not including school board member or officer, and shall not have served as an officer of a political party, or served as a registered paid lobbyist or as an officer of a candidate's campaign committee.

(4) The commission on appellate court appointments shall nominate candidates for appointment to the independent redistricting commission, except that, if a politically balanced commission exists whose members are nominated by the commission on appellate court appointments and whose regular duties relate to the elective process, the commission on appellate court appointments may delegate to such existing commission (hereinafter called the commission on appellate court appointments' designee) the duty of nominating members for the independent redistricting commission, and all other duties assigned to the commission on appellate court appointments in this section.

(5) By January 8 of years ending in one, the commission on appellate court appointments or its designee shall establish a pool of persons who are willing to serve on and are qualified for appointment to the independent redistricting commission. The pool of candidates shall consist of twenty-five nominees, with ten nominees from each of the two largest political parties in Arizona based on party registration, and five who are not registered with either of the two largest political parties in Arizona.

(6) Appointments to the independent redistricting commission shall be made in the order set forth below. No later than January 31 of years ending in one, the highest ranking officer elected by the Arizona house of representatives shall make one appointment to the independent redistricting commission from the pool of nominees, followed by one appointment from the pool made in turn by each of the following: the minority party leader of the Arizona house of representatives, the highest ranking officer elected by the Arizona senate, and the minority party leader of the Arizona senate. Each such official shall have a seven-day period in which to make an appointment. Any official who fails to make an appointment within the specified time period will forfeit the appointment privilege. In the event that there are two or more minority parties within the house or the senate, the leader of the largest minority party by statewide party registration shall make the appointment.

(7) Any vacancy in the above four independent redistricting commission positions remaining as of March 1 of a year ending in one shall be filled from the pool of nominees by the commission on appellate court appointments or its designee. The appointing body shall strive for political balance and fairness.

(8) At a meeting called by the secretary of state, the four independent redistricting commission members shall select by majority vote from the nomination pool a fifth member who shall not be registered with any party already represented on the independent redistricting commission and who shall serve as chair. If the four commissioners fail to appoint a fifth member within fifteen days, the commission on appellate court appointments or its designee, striving for political balance and fairness, shall appoint a fifth member from the nomination pool, who shall serve as chair.

(9) The five commissioners shall then select by majority vote one of their members to serve as vice-chair.

(10) After having been served written notice and provided with an opportunity for a response, a member of the independent redistricting commission may be removed by the governor, with the concurrence of two-thirds of the senate, for substantial neglect of duty, gross misconduct in office, or inability to discharge the duties of office.

(11) If a commissioner or chair does not complete the term of office for any reason, the commission on appellate court appointments or its designee shall nominate a pool of three candidates within the first thirty days after the vacancy occurs. The nominees shall be of the same political party or status as was the member who vacated the office at the time of his or her appointment, and the appointment other than the chair shall be made by the current holder of the office designated to make the original appointment. The appointment of a new chair shall be made by the remaining commissioners. If the appointment of a replacement commissioner or chair is not made within fourteen days following the presentation of the nominees, the commission on appellate court appointments or its designee shall make the appointment, striving for political balance and fairness. The newly appointed commissioner shall serve out the remainder of the original term.

(12) Three commissioners, including the chair or vice-chair, constitute a quorum. Three or more affirmative votes are required for any official action. Where a quorum is present, the independent redistricting commission shall conduct business in meetings open to the public, with 48 or more hours public notice provided.

(13) A commissioner, during the commissioner's term of office and for three years thereafter, shall be ineligible for Arizona public office or for registration as a paid lobbyist.

(14) The independent redistricting commission shall establish congressional and legislative districts. The commencement of the mapping process for both the congressional and legislative districts shall be the creation of districts of equal population in a grid-like pattern across the state. Adjustments to the grid shall then be made as necessary to accommodate the goals as set forth below:

A. Districts shall comply with the United States Constitution and the United States voting rights act;

B. Congressional districts shall have equal population to the extent practicable, and state legislative districts shall have equal population to the extent practicable;

C. Districts shall be geographically compact and contiguous to the extent practicable;

D. District boundaries shall respect communities of interest to the extent practicable;

E. To the extent practicable, district lines shall use visible geographic features, city, town and county boundaries, and undivided census tracts;

F. To the extent practicable, competitive districts should be favored where to do so would create no significant detriment to the other goals.

(15) Party registration and voting history data shall be excluded from the initial phase of the mapping process but may be used to test maps for compliance with the above goals. The places of residence of incumbents or candidates shall not be identified or considered.

(16) The independent redistricting commission shall advertise a draft map of congressional districts and a draft map of legislative districts to the public for comment, which comment shall be taken for at least thirty days. Either or both bodies of the legislature may act within this period to make recommendations to the independent redistricting commission by memorial or by minority report, which recommendations shall be considered by the independent redistricting commission. The independent redistricting commission shall then establish final district boundaries.

(17) The provisions regarding this section are self-executing. The independent redistricting commission shall certify to the secretary of state the establishment of congressional and legislative districts.

(18) Upon approval of this amendment, the department of administration or its successor shall make adequate office space available for the independent redistricting commission. The treasurer of the state shall make $6,000,000 available for the work of the independent redistricting commission pursuant to the year 2000 census. Unused monies shall be returned to the state's general fund. In years ending in eight or nine after the year 2001, the department of administration or its successor shall submit to the legislature a recommendation for an appropriation for adequate redistricting expenses and shall make available adequate office space for the operation of the independent redistricting commission. The legislature shall make the necessary appropriations by a majority vote.

(19) The independent redistricting commission, with fiscal oversight from the department of administration or its successor, shall have procurement and contracting authority and may hire staff and consultants for the purposes of this section, including legal representation.

(20) The independent redistricting commission shall have standing in legal actions regarding the redistricting plan and the adequacy of resources provided for the operation of the independent redistricting commission. The independent redistricting commission shall have sole authority to determine whether the Arizona attorney general or counsel hired or selected by the independent redistricting commission shall represent the people of Arizona in the legal defense of a redistricting plan.

(21) Members of the independent redistricting commission are eligible for reimbursement of expenses pursuant to law, and a member's residence is deemed to be the member's post of duty for purposes of reimbursement of expenses.

(22) Employees of the department of administration or its successor shall not influence or attempt to influence the district-mapping decisions of the independent redistricting commission.

(23) Each commissioner's duties established by this section expire upon the appointment of the first member of the next redistricting commission. The independent redistricting commission shall not meet or incur expenses after the redistricting plan is completed, except if litigation or any government approval of the plan is pending, or to revise districts if required by court decisions or if the number of congressional or legislative districts is changed.

Section 2. Qualifications of members of legislature

No person shall be a member of the Legislature unless he shall be a citizen of the United States at the time of his election, nor unless he shall be at least twenty-five years of age, and shall have been a resident of Arizona at least three years and of the county from which he is elected at least one year before his election.

Section 3. Sessions of legislature; special sessions; limitation of subjects for consideration

The sessions of the legislature shall be held annually at the capitol of the state, and shall commence on the second Monday of January of each year. The governor may call a special session, whenever in his judgment it is advisable. In calling a special session, the governor shall specify the subjects to be considered, and at such special session no laws shall be enacted except such as relate to the subjects mentioned in the call.

Section 4. Disqualification for membership in Legislature

No person holding any public office of profit or trust under the authority of the United States, or of this state, shall be a member of the legislature; Provided, that appointments in the state militia and the offices of notary public, justice of the peace, United States commissioner, and postmaster of the fourth class, shall not work disqualification for membership within the meaning of this section.

Section 5. Ineligibility of members of legislature to other public offices

No member of the legislature, during the term for which he shall have been elected or appointed shall be eligible to hold any other office or be otherwise employed by the state of Arizona or, any county or incorporated city or town thereof. This prohibition shall not extend to the office of school trustee, nor to employment as a teacher or instructor in the public school system.

Section 6. Privilege from arrest; civil process

Members of the legislature shall be privileged from arrest in all cases except treason, felony, and breach of the peace, and they shall not be subject to any civil process during the session of the legislature, nor for fifteen days next before the commencement of each session.

Section 7. Freedom of debate

No member of the legislature shall be liable in any civil or criminal prosecution for words spoken in debate.

Section 8. Organization; officers; rules of procedure

Each house, when assembled, shall choose its own officers, judge of the election and qualification of its own members, and determine its own rules of procedure.

Section 9. Quorum; compelling attendance; adjournment

The majority of the members of each house shall constitute a quorum to do business, but a smaller number may meet, adjourn from day to day, and compel the attendance of absent members, in such manner and under such penalties as each house may prescribe. Neither house shall adjourn for more than three days, nor to any place other than that in which it may be sitting, without the consent of the other.

Section 10. Journal of proceedings; roll call

Each house shall keep a journal of its proceedings, and at the request of two members the ayes and nays on roll call on any question shall be entered.

Section 11. Disorderly behavior; expulsion of members

Each house may punish its members for disorderly behavior, and may, with the concurrence of two-thirds of its members, expel any member.

Section 12. Procedure on bills; approval or disapproval by governor

Every bill shall be read by sections on three different days, unless in case of emergency, two-thirds of either house deem it expedient to dispense with this rule. The vote on the final passage of any bill or joint resolution shall be taken by ayes and nays on roll call. Every measure when finally passed shall be presented to the governor for his approval or disapproval.

Section 13. Subject and title of bills

Every act shall embrace but one subject and matters properly connected therewith, which subject shall be expressed in the title; but if any subject shall be embraced in an act which shall not be expressed in the title, such act shall be void only as to so much thereof as shall not be embraced in the title.

Section 14. Legislation by reference prohibited

No Act or section thereof shall be revised or amended by mere reference to the title of such act, but the act or section as amended shall be set forth and published at full length.

Section 15. Passage of bills by majority; signing of bills

A majority of all members elected to each house shall be necessary to pass any bill, and all bills so passed shall be signed by the presiding officer of each house in open session.

Section 16. Right to protest

Any member of the legislature shall have the right to protest and have the reasons of his protest entered on the journal.

Section 17. Extra compensation prohibited; increase or decrease of compensation during term of office

The legislature shall never grant any extra compensation to any public officer, agent, servant or contractor, after the services shall have been rendered or the contract entered into, nor shall the compensation of any public officer, other than a justice of the peace, be increased or diminished during his term of office; provided, however, that when any legislative increase or decrease in compensation of the members of any court or the clerk thereof, or of any board or commission composed of two or more officers or persons whose respective terms of office are not coterminous, has heretofore or shall hereafter become effective as to any member or clerk of such court, or any member of such board or commission, it shall be effective from such date as to each thereof.

Section 18. Suits against state

The legislature shall direct by law in what manner and in what courts suits may be brought against the state.

Section 19. Local or special laws

No local or special laws shall be enacted in any of the following cases, that is to say:

1. Granting divorces.

2. Locating or changing county seats.

3. Changing rules of evidence.

4. Changing the law of descent or succession.

5. Regulating the practice of courts of justice.

6. Limitation of civil actions or giving effect to informal or invalid deeds.

7. Punishment of crimes and misdemeanors.

8. Laying out, opening, altering, or vacating roads, plats, streets, alleys, and public squares.

9. Assessment and collection of taxes.

10. Regulating the rate of interest on money.

11. The conduct of elections.

12. Affecting the estates of deceased persons or of minors.

13. Granting to any corporation, association, or individual, any special or exclusive privileges, immunities, or franchises.

14. Remitting fines, penalties, and forfeitures.

15. Changing names of persons or places.

16. Regulating the jurisdiction and duties of justices of the peace.

17. Incorporation of cities, towns, or villages, or amending their charters.

18. Relinquishing any indebtedness, liability, or obligation to this State.

19. Summoning and empanelling of juries.

20. When a general law can be made applicable.

Section 20. Appropriation bills

The general appropriation bill shall embrace nothing but appropriations for the different departments of the state, for state institutions, for public schools, and for interest on the public debt. All other appropriations shall be made by separate bills, each embracing but one subject.

Section 21. Term limits of members of state legislature

The members of the first legislature shall hold office until the first Monday in January, 1913. The terms of office of the members of succeeding legislatures shall be two years. No state senator shall serve more than four consecutive terms in that office, nor shall any state representative serve more than four consecutive terms in that office. This limitation on the number of terms of consecutive service shall apply to terms of office beginning on or after January 1, 1993. No legislator, after serving the maximum number of terms, which shall include any part of a term served, may serve in the same office until he has been out of office for no less than one full term.

Section 22. Juvenile justice; certain chronic and violent juvenile offenders prosecuted as adults; community alternatives for certain juvenile offenders; public proceedings and records

In order to preserve and protect the right of the people to justice and public safety, and to ensure fairness and accountability when juveniles engage in unlawful conduct, the legislature, or the people by initiative or referendum, shall have the authority to enact substantive and procedural laws regarding all proceedings and matters affecting such juveniles. The following rights, duties, and powers shall govern such proceedings and matters:

1. Juveniles 15 years of age or older accused of murder, forcible sexual assault, armed robbery or other violent felony offenses as defined by statute shall be prosecuted as adults. Juveniles 15 years of age or older who are chronic felony offenders as defined by statute shall be prosecuted as adults. Upon conviction all such juveniles shall be subject to the same laws as adults, except as specifically provided by statute and by article XXII, section 16 of this constitution. All other juveniles accused of unlawful conduct shall be prosecuted as provided by law. Every juvenile convicted of or found responsible for unlawful conduct shall make prompt restitution to any victims of such conduct for their injury or loss.

2. County attorneys shall have the authority to defer the prosecution of juveniles who are not accused of violent offenses and who are not chronic felony offenders as defined by statute and to establish community-based alternatives for resolving matters involving such juveniles.

3. All proceedings and matters involving juveniles accused of unlawful conduct shall be open to the public and all records of those proceedings shall be public records. Exceptions shall be made only for the protection of the privacy of innocent victims of crime, or when a court of competent jurisdiction finds a clear public interest in confidentiality.

Section 23. Passes and purchase of transportation by public officers;inapplication to national guard

It shall not be lawful for any person holding public office in this state to accept or use a pass or to purchase transportation from any railroad or other corporation, other than as such transportation may be purchased by the general public; Provided, that this shall not apply to members of the national guard of Arizona traveling under orders. The legislature shall enact laws to enforce this provision.

Section 24. Enacting clause of bills; initiative bills

The enacting clause of every bill enacted by the legislature shall be as follows: "Be it enacted by the Legislature of the State of Arizona," or when the initiative is used: "Be it enacted by the People of the State of Arizona."

Section 25. Continuity of governmental operations in emergency

The legislature, in order to insure continuity of state and local governmental operations in periods of emergency resulting from disasters caused by enemy attack, shall have the power and the immediate duty to:

1. Provide for prompt and temporary succession to the powers and duties of public offices, of whatever nature and whether filled by election or appointment, the incumbents of which may become unavailable for carrying on the powers and duties of such offices.

2. Adopt such other measures as may be necessary and proper for insuring the continuity of governmental operations.

In the exercise of the powers hereby conferred, the legislature shall in all respects conform to the requirements of this constitution except to the extent that in the judgment of the legislature so to do would be impracticable or would admit of undue delay.

Article V: Executive Department

Section 1. Executive department; state officers; terms; election; residence and office at seat of government; duties

A. The executive department shall consist of the governor, secretary of state, state treasurer, attorney general, and superintendent of public instruction, each of whom shall hold office for four years beginning on the first Monday of January, 1971 next after the regular general election in 1970.

B. The person having the highest number of the votes cast for the office voted for shall be elected, but if two or more persons have an equal and the highest number of votes for the office, the two houses of the legislature at its next regular session shall elect forthwith, by joint ballot, one of such persons for said office.

C. The officers of the executive department during their terms of office shall reside at the seat of government where they shall keep their offices and the public records, books, and papers. They shall perform such duties as are prescribed by the constitution and as may be provided by law.

Section 1. Term limits on executive department and state officers; term lengths; election; residence and office at seat of government; duties

A. The executive department shall consist of the governor, secretary of state, state treasurer, attorney general, and superintendent of public instruction, each of whom shall hold office for a term of four years beginning on the first Monday of January, 1971 next after the regular general election in 1970. No member of the executive department shall hold that office for more than two consecutive terms. This limitation on the number of terms of consecutive service shall apply to terms of office beginning on or after January 1, 1993. No member of the executive department after serving the maximum number of terms, which shall include any part of a term served, may serve in the same office until out of office for no less than one full term.

B. The person having a majority of the votes cast for the office voted for shall be elected. If no person receives a majority of the votes cast for the office, a second election shall be held as prescribed by law between the persons receiving the highest and second highest number of votes cast for the office. The person receiving the highest number of votes at the second election for the office is elected, but if the two persons have an equal number of votes for the office, the two houses of the legislature at its next regular session shall elect forthwith, by joint ballot, one of such persons for said office.

C. The officers of the executive department during their terms of office shall reside at the seat of government where they shall keep their offices and the public records, books, and papers. They shall perform such duties as are prescribed by the constitution and as may be provided by law.

Section 2. Eligibility to state offices

No person shall be eligible to any of the offices mentioned in section 1 of this article except a person of the age of not less than twenty-five years, who shall have been for ten years next preceding his election a citizen of the United States, and for five years next preceding his election a citizen of Arizona.

Section 3. Governor, commander-in-chief of the military forces

The governor shall be commander-in-chief of the military forces of the state, except when such forces shall be called into the service of the United States.

Section 4. Governor; powers and duties; special sessions of legislature; message and recommendations

The governor shall transact all executive business with the officers of the government, civil and military, and may require information in writing from the officers in the executive department upon any subject relating to the duties of their respective offices. He shall take care that the laws be faithfully executed. He may convene the legislature in extraordinary session. He shall communicate, by message, to the legislature at every session the condition of the state, and recommend such matters as he shall deem expedient.

Section 5. Reprieves, commutations and pardons

The governor shall have power to grant reprieves, commutation, and pardons, after convictions, for all offenses except treason and cases of impeachment, upon such conditions and with such restrictions and limitations as may be provided by law.

Section 6. Death, resignation, removal or disability of governor; succession to office; impeachment, absence from state or temporary disability

In the event of the death of the governor, or his resignation, removal from office, or permanent disability to discharge the duties of the office, the secretary of state, if holding by election, shall succeed to the office of governor until his successor shall be elected and shall qualify. If the secretary of state be holding otherwise than by election, or shall fail to qualify as governor, the attorney general, the state treasurer, or the superintendent of public instruction, if holding by election, shall, in the order named, succeed to the office of governor. The taking of the oath of office as governor by any person specified in this section shall constitute resignation from the office by virtue of the holding of which he qualifies as governor. Any successor to the office shall become governor in fact and entitled to all of the emoluments, powers and duties of governor upon taking the oath of office.

In the event of the impeachment of the governor, his absence from the state, or other temporary disability to discharge the duties of the office, the powers and duties of the office of governor shall devolve upon the same person as in case of vacancy, but only until the disability ceases.

Section 7. Presentation of bills to governor; approval; veto; filing with secretary of state; veto of items in appropriation bills; inapplication of veto power to referred bills

Every bill passed by the legislature, before it becomes a law, shall be presented to the governor. If he approve, he shall sign it, and it shall become a law as provided in this constitution. But if he disapprove, he shall return it, with his objections, to the house in which it originated, which shall enter the objections at large on the journal. If after reconsideration it again passes both houses by an aye and nay vote on roll call of two-thirds of the members elected to each house, it shall become a law as provided in this constitution, notwithstanding the governor's objections. This section shall not apply to emergency measures as referred to in section 1 of the article on the legislative department.

If any bill be not returned within five days after it shall have been presented to the governor (Sunday excepted) such bill shall become a law in like manner as if he had signed it, unless the legislature by its final adjournment prevents its return, in which case it shall be filed with his objections in the office of the secretary of state within ten days after such adjournment (Sundays excepted) or become a law as provided in this constitution. After the final action by the governor, or following the adoption of a bill notwithstanding his objection, it shall be filed with the secretary of state.

If any bill presented to the governor contains several items of appropriations of money, he may object to one or more of such items, while approving other portions of the bill. In such case he shall append to the bill at the time of signing it, a statement of the item or items which he declines to approve, together with his reasons therefor, and such item or items shall not take effect unless passed over the governor's objections as in this section provided.

The veto power of the governor shall not extend to any bill passed by the legislature and referred to the people for adoption or rejection.

Section 8. Vacancies in office

When any office shall, from any cause, become vacant, and no mode shall be provided by the Constitution or by law for filling such vacancy, the governor shall have the power to fill such vacancy by appointment.

Section 9. Powers and duties of state officers

The powers and duties of secretary of state, state treasurer, attorney-general, and superintendent of public instruction shall be as prescribed by law.

Section 10. Canvass of election returns for state officers; certificates of election

The returns of the election for all state officers shall be canvassed, and certificates of election issued by the secretary of state, in such manner as may be provided by law.

Section 11. Commissions

All commissions shall issue in the name of the state, and shall be signed by the governor, sealed with the seal of the state, and attested by the secretary of state.

Section 12. Compensation of elective state officers; commission on salaries for elective state officers

The salaries of those holding elective state offices shall be as established by law from time to time, subject to the limitations of article VI, section 33 and to the limitations of article IV, part 2, section 17. Such salaries as are presently established may be altered from time to time by the procedure established in this section or as otherwise provided by law, except that legislative salaries may be altered only by the procedures established in this section.

A commission to be known as the commission on salaries for elective state officers is authorized to be established by the legislature. The commission shall be composed of five members appointed from private life, two of whom shall be appointed by the governor and one each by the president of the senate, the speaker of the house of representatives, and the chief justice. At such times as may be directed by the legislature, the commission shall report to the governor with recommendations concerning the rates of pay of elected state officers. The governor shall upon the receipt of such report make recommendations to the legislature with respect to the exact rates of pay which he deems advisable for those offices and positions other than for the rates of pay of members of the legislature. Such recommendations shall become effective at a time established by the legislature after the transmission of the recommendation of the governor without aid of further legislative action unless, within such period of time, there has been enacted into law a statute which establishes rates of pay other than those proposed by the governor, or unless either house of the legislature specifically disapproves all or part of the governor's recommendation. The recommendations of the governor, unless disapproved or altered within the time provided by law, shall be effective; and any 1971 recommendations shall be effective as to all offices on the first Monday in January of 1973. In case of either a legislative enactment or disapproval by either house, the recommendations shall be effective only insofar as not altered or disapproved. The recommendations of the commission as to legislative salaries shall be certified by it to the secretary of state and the secretary of state shall submit to the qualified electors at the next regular general election the question, "Shall the recommendations of the commission on salaries for elective state officers concerning legislative salaries be accepted? [ ] Yes [ ] No." Such recommendations if approved by the electors shall become effective at the beginning of the next regular legislative session without any other authorizing legislation. All recommendations which become effective under this section shall supersede all laws enacted prior to their effective date relating to such salaries.

Article VI: Judicial Department

Section 1. Judicial power; courts

The judicial power shall be vested in an integrated judicial department consisting of a supreme court, such intermediate appellate courts as may be provided by law, a superior court, such courts inferior to the superior court as may be provided by law, and justice courts.

Section 2. Supreme court; composition; divisions; decisions, transaction of business

The supreme court shall consist of not less than five justices. The number of justices may be increased or decreased by law, but the court shall at all times be constituted of at least five justices.

The supreme court shall sit in accordance with rules adopted by it, either in banc or in divisions of not less than three justices, but the court shall not declare any law unconstitutional except when sitting in banc. The decisions of the court shall be in writing and the grounds stated.

The court shall be open at all times, except on nonjudicial days, for the transaction of business.

Section 3. Supreme court; administrative supervision; chief justice

The supreme court shall have administrative supervision over all the courts of the state. The chief justice shall be elected by the justices of the supreme court from one of their number for a term of five years, and may be reelected for like terms. The vice chief justice shall be elected by the justices of the supreme court from one of their number for a term determined by the court. A member of the court may resign the office of chief justice or vice chief justice without resigning from the court.

The chief justice, or in his absence or incapacity, the vice chief justice, shall exercise the court's administrative supervision over all the courts of the state. He may assign judges of intermediate appellate courts, superior courts, or courts inferior to the superior court to serve in other courts or counties.

Section 4. Supreme court; term of office

Justices of the supreme court shall hold office for a regular term of six years except as provided by this article.

Section 5. Supreme court; jurisdiction; writs; rules; habeas corpus

The supreme court shall have:

1. Original jurisdiction of habeas corpus, and quo warranto, mandamus, injunction and other extraordinary writs to state officers.

2. Original and exclusive jurisdiction to hear and determine causes between counties concerning disputed boundaries and surveys thereof or concerning claims of one county against another.

3. Appellate jurisdiction in all actions and proceedings except civil and criminal actions originating in courts not of record, unless the action involves the validity of a tax, impost, assessment, toll, statute or municipal ordinance.

4. Power to issue injunctions and writs of mandamus, review, prohibition, habeas corpus, certiorari, and all other writs necessary and proper to the complete exercise of its appellate and revisory jurisdiction.

5. Power to make rules relative to all procedural matters in any court.

6. Such other jurisdiction as may be provided by law.

Each justice of the supreme court may issue writs of habeas corpus to any part of the state upon petition by or on behalf of a person held in actual custody, and may make such writs returnable before himself, the supreme court, appellate court or superior court, or judge thereof.

Section 6. Supreme court; qualifications of justices

A justice of the supreme court shall be a person of good moral character and admitted to the practice of law in and a resident of the state of Arizona for ten years next preceding his taking office.

Section 7. Supreme court; clerk and assistants; administrative director and staff

The supreme court shall appoint a clerk of the court and assistants thereto who shall serve at its pleasure, and who shall receive such compensation as may be provided by law.

The supreme court shall appoint an administrative director and staff to serve at its pleasure to assist the chief justice in discharging his administrative duties. The director and staff shall receive such compensation as may be provided by law.

Section 8. Supreme court; publication of opinions

Provision shall be made by law for the speedy publication of the opinions of the supreme court, and they shall be free for publication by any person.

Section 9. Intermediate appellate courts

The jurisdiction, powers, duties and composition of any intermediate appellate court shall be as provided by law.

Section 10. Superior court; number of judges

There shall be in each county at least one judge of the superior court. There shall be in each county such additional judges as may be provided by law, but not exceeding one judge for each thirty thousand inhabitants or majority fraction thereof. The number of inhabitants in a county for purposes of this section may be determined by census enumeration or by such other method as may be provided by law.

Section 11. Superior court; presiding judges; duties

There shall be in each county a presiding judge of the superior court. In each county in which there are two or more judges, the supreme court shall appoint one of such judges presiding judge. Presiding judges shall exercise administrative supervision over the superior court and judges thereof in their counties, and shall have such other duties as may be provided by law or by rules of the supreme court.

Section 12. Superior court; term of office

A. Judges of the superior court in counties having a population of less than two hundred fifty thousand persons according to the most recent United States census shall be elected by the qualified electors of their counties at the general election. They shall hold office for a regular term of four years except as provided by this section from and after the first Monday in January next succeeding their election, and until their successors are elected and qualify. The names of all candidates for judge of the superior court in such counties shall be placed on the regular ballot without partisan or other designation except the division and title of the office.

B. The governor shall fill any vacancy in such counties by appointing a person to serve until the election and qualification of a successor. At the next succeeding general election following the appointment of a person to fill a vacancy, a judge shall be elected to serve for the remainder of the unexpired term.

Judges of the superior court in counties having a population of two hundred fifty thousand persons or more according to the most recent United States census shall hold office for a regular term of four years except as provided by this article.

Section 13. Superior court; composition; salaries; judgments and proceedings; process

The superior courts provided for in this article shall constitute a single court, composed of all the duly elected or appointed judges in each of the counties of the state. The legislature may classify counties for the purpose of fixing salaries of judges or officers of the court.

The judgments, decrees, orders and proceedings of any session of the superior court held by one or more judges shall have the same force and effect as if all the judges of the court had presided.

The process of the court shall extend to all parts of the state.

Section 14. Superior court; original jurisdiction

The superior court shall have original jurisdiction of:

1. Cases and proceedings in which exclusive jurisdiction is not vested by law in another court.

2. Cases of equity and at law which involve the title to or possession of real property, or the legality of any tax, impost, assessment, toll or municipal ordinance.

3. Other cases in which the demand or value of property in controversy amounts to one thousand dollars or more, exclusive of interest and costs.

4. Criminal cases amounting to felony, and cases of misdemeanor not otherwise provided for by law.

5. Actions of forcible entry and detainer.

6. Proceedings in insolvency.

7. Actions to prevent or abate nuisance.

8. Matters of probate.

9. Divorce and for annulment of marriage.

10. Naturalization and the issuance of papers therefor.

11. Special cases and proceedings not otherwise provided for, and such other jurisdiction as may be provided by law.

Section 15. Jurisdiction and authority in juvenile proceedings

The jurisdiction and authority of the courts of this state in all proceedings and matters affecting juveniles shall be as provided by the legislature or the people by initiative or referendum.

Section 16. Superior court; appellate jurisdiction

The superior court shall have appellate jurisdiction in cases arising in justice and other courts inferior to the superior court as may be provided by law.

Section 17. Superior court; conduct of business; trial juries; jury trial; grand juries

The superior court shall be open at all times, except on nonjudicial days, for the determination of non-jury civil cases and the transaction of business. For the determination of civil causes and matters in which a jury demand has been entered, and for the trial of criminal causes, a trial jury shall be drawn and summoned from the body of the county, as provided by law. The right of jury trial as provided by this constitution shall remain inviolate, but trial by jury may be waived by the parties in any civil cause or by the parties with the consent of the court in any criminal cause. Grand juries shall be drawn and summoned only by order of the superior court.

Section 18. Superior court; writs

The superior court or any judge thereof may issue writs of mandamus, quo warranto, review, certiorari, prohibition, and writs of habeas corpus on petition by or on behalf of a person held in actual custody within the county. Injunctions, attachments, and writs of prohibition and habeas corpus may be issued and served on legal holidays and non-judicial days.

Section 19. Superior court; service of judge in another county

A judge of the superior court shall serve in another county at the direction of the chief justice of the supreme court or may serve in another county at the request of the presiding judge of the superior court thereof.

Section 20. Retirement and service of retired justices and judges

The legislature shall prescribe by law a plan of retirement for justices and judges of courts of record, including the basis and amount of retirement pay, and requiring except as provided in section 35 of this article, that justices and judges of courts of record be retired upon reaching the age of seventy. Any retired justice or judge of any court of record who is drawing retirement pay may serve as a justice or judge of any court. When serving outside his county of residence, any such retired justice or judge shall receive his necessary traveling and subsistence expenses. A retired judge who is temporarily called back to the active duties of a judge is entitled to receive the same compensation and expenses as other like active judges less any amount received for such period in retirement benefits.

Section 21. Superior court; speedy decisions

Every matter submitted to a judge of the superior court for his decision shall be decided within sixty days from the date of submission thereof. The supreme court shall by rule provide for the speedy disposition of all matters not decided within such period.

Section 22. Superior and other courts; qualifications of judges

Judges of the superior court, intermediate appellate courts or courts inferior to the superior court having jurisdiction in civil cases of one thousand dollars or more, exclusive of interest and costs, established by law under the provisions of section 1 of this article, shall be at least thirty years of age, of good moral character and admitted to the practice of law in and a resident of the state for five years next preceding their taking office.

Section 23. Superior court; clerk

There shall be in each county a clerk of the superior court. The clerk shall be elected by the qualified electors of his county at the general election and shall hold office for a term of four years from and after the first Monday in January next succeeding his election. The clerk shall have such powers and perform such duties as may be provided by law or by rule of the supreme court or superior court. He shall receive such compensation as may be provided by law.

Section 24. Superior court; court commissioners, masters and referees

Judges of the superior court may appoint court commissioners, masters and referees in their respective counties, who shall have such powers and perform such duties as may be provided by law or by rule of the supreme court. Court commissioners, masters and referees shall receive such compensation as may be provided by law.

Section 25. Style of process; conduct of prosecutions in name of state

The style of process shall be "The State of Arizona", and prosecutions shall be conducted in the name of the state and by its authority.

Section 26. Oath of office

Each justice, judge and justice of the peace shall, before entering upon the duties of his office, take and subscribe an oath that he will support the Constitution of the United States and the Constitution of the State of Arizona, and that he will faithfully and impartially discharge the duties of his office to the best of his ability.

The oath of all judges of courts inferior to the superior court and the oath of justices of the peace shall be filed in the office of the county recorder, and the oath of all other justices and judges shall be filed in the office of the secretary of state.

Section 27. Charge to juries; reversal of causes for technical error

Judges shall not charge juries with respect to matters of fact, nor comment thereon, but shall declare the law. No cause shall be reversed for technical error in pleadings or proceedings when upon the whole case it shall appear that substantial justice has been done.

Section 28. Justices and judges; dual office holding; political activity; practice of law

Justices and judges of courts of record shall not be eligible for any other public office or for any other public employment during their term of office, except that they may assume another judicial office, and upon qualifying therefor, the office formerly held shall become vacant. No justice or judge of any court of record shall practice law during his continuance in office, nor shall he hold any office in a political party or actively take part in any political campaign other than his own for his reelection or retention in office. Any justice or judge who files nomination papers for an elective office, other than for judge of the superior court or a court of record inferior to the superior court in a county having a population of less than two hundred fifty thousand persons according to the most recent United States census, forfeits his judicial office.

Section 30. Courts of record

A. The supreme court, the court of appeals and the superior court shall be courts of record. Other courts of record may be established by law, but justice courts shall not be courts of record.

B. All justices and judges of courts of record, except for judges of the superior court and other courts of record inferior to the superior court in counties having a population of less than two hundred fifty thousand persons according to the most recent United States census, shall be appointed in the manner provided in section 37 of this article.

Section 31. Judges pro tempore

A. The legislature may provide for the appointment of members of the bar having the qualifications provided in section 22 of this article as judges pro tempore of courts inferior to the supreme court, except that justices of the peace pro tempore shall have the same qualifications as justices of the peace and do not have to reside in the precinct in which the justice of the peace pro tempore is appointed to serve.

B. When serving, any such person shall have all the judicial powers of a regular elected judge of the court to which the person is appointed. A person so appointed shall receive such compensation as may be provided by law. The population limitation of section 10 of this article shall not apply to the appointment of judges pro tempore of the superior court.

Section 32. Justices of the peace and inferior courts; jurisdiction, powers and duties; terms of office; salaries

A. The number of justices of the peace to be elected in precincts shall be as provided by law. Justices of the peace may be police justices of incorporated cities and towns.

B. The jurisdiction, powers and duties of courts inferior to the superior court and of justice courts, and the terms of office of judges of such courts and justices of the peace shall be as provided by law. The legislature may classify counties and precincts for the purpose of fixing salaries of judges of courts inferior to the superior court and of justices of the peace.

C. The civil jurisdiction of courts inferior to the superior court and of justice courts shall not exceed the sum of ten thousand dollars, exclusive of interest and costs. Criminal jurisdiction shall be limited to misdemeanors. The jurisdiction of such courts shall not encroach upon the jurisdiction of courts of record but may be made concurrent therewith, subject to the limitations provided in this section.

Section 33. Change by legislature in number of justices or judges; reduction of salary during term of office

No change made by the legislature in the number of justices or judges shall work the removal of any justice or judge from office. The salary of any justice or judge shall not be reduced during the term of office for which he was elected or appointed.

Section 34. Absence of judicial officer from state

Any judicial officer except a retired justice or judge who absents himself from the state for more than sixty consecutive days shall be deemed to have forfeited his office, but the governor may extend the leave of absence for such time as reasonable necessity therefor exists.

Section 35. Continuance in office; continued existence of offices; application of prior statute and rules

A. All justices judges, justices of the peace and officers of any court who are holding office as such by election or appointment at the time of the adoption of this section shall serve or continue in office for the respective terms for which they are so elected or for their respective unexpired terms, and until their successors are elected or appointed and qualify or they are retained in office pursuant to section 38 of this article; provided, however, that any justice or judge elected at the general election at which this section is adopted shall serve for the term for which he is so elected. The continued existence of any office heretofore legally established or held shall not be abolished or repealed by the adoption of this article. The statutes and rules relating to the authority, jurisdiction, practice and procedure of courts, judicial officers and offices in force at the time of the adoption of this article and not inconsistent herewith, shall, so far as applicable, apply to and govern such courts, judicial officers and offices until amended or repealed.

B. All judges of the superior court holding office by appointment or retention in counties with a population of two hundred fifty thousand persons or more according to the most recent United States census at the time of the adoption of this amendment to this section shall serve or continue in office for the respective terms for which they were appointed. Upon an incumbent vacating the office of judge of the superior court, whether by failing to file a declaration for retention, by rejection by the qualified electors of the county or resignation, the appointment shall be pursuant to section 37 of this article.

Section 36. Commission on appellate court appointments and terms, appointments and vacancies on commission

A. There shall be a nonpartisan commission on appellate court appointments which shall be composed of the chief justice of the supreme court, who shall be chairman, five attorney members, who shall be nominated by the board of governors of the state bar of Arizona and appointed by the governor with the advice and consent of the senate in the manner prescribed by law, and ten nonatto rney members who shall be appointed by the governor with the advice and consent of the senate in the manner prescribed by law. At least ninety days prior to a term expiring or within twenty-one days of a vacancy occurring for a nonattorney member on the commission for appellate court appointments, the governor shall appoint a nominating committee of nine members, not more than five of whom may be from the same political party. The makeup of the committee shall, to the extent feasible, reflect the diversity of the population of the state. Members shall not be attorneys and shall not hold any governmental office, elective or appointive, for profit. The committee shall provide public notice that a vacancy exists and shall solicit, review and forward to the governor all applications along with the committee's recommendations for appointment.

Attorney members of the commission shall have resided in the state and shall have been admitted to practice before the supreme court for not less than five years. Not more than three attorney members shall be members of the same political party and not more than two attorney members shall be residents of any one county. Nonattorney members shall have resided in the state for not less than five years and shall not be judges, retired judges or admitted to practice before the supreme court. Not more than five nonattorney members shall be members of the same political party. Not more than two nonattorney members shall be residents of any one county. None of the attorney or nonattorney members of the commission shall hold any governmental office, elective or appointive, for profit, and no attorney member shall be eligible for appointment to any judicial office of the state until one year after he ceases to be a member. Attorney members of the commission shall serve staggered four-year terms and nonattorney members shall serve staggered four-year terms. Vacancies shall be filled for the unexpired terms in the same manner as the original appointments.

B. No person other than the chief justice shall serve at the same time as a member of more than one judicial appointment commission.

C. In making or confirming appointments to the appellate court commission, the governor, the senate and the state bar shall endeavor to see that the commission reflects the diversity of Arizona's population.

In the event of the absence or incapacity of the chairman the supreme court shall appoint a justice thereof to serve in his place and stead.

D. Prior to making recommendations to the governor as hereinafter provided, the commission shall conduct investigations, hold public hearings and take public testimony. An executive session as prescribed by rule may be held upon a two-thirds vote of the members of the commission in a public hearing. Final decisions as to recommendations shall be made without regard to political affiliation in an impartial and objective manner. The commission shall consider the diversity of the state's population, however the primary consideration shall be merit. Voting shall be in a public hearing. The expenses of meetings of the commission and the attendance of members thereof for travel and subsistence shall be paid from the general fund of the state as state officers are paid, upon claims approved by the chairman.

E. After public hearings the supreme court shall adopt rules of procedure for the commission on appellate court appointments.

F. Notwithstanding the provisions of subsection A, the initial appointments for the five additional nonattorney members and the two additional attorney members of the commission shall be designated by the governor for staggered terms as follows:

1. One appointment for a nonattorney member shall be for a one-year term.

2. Two appointments for nonattorney members shall be for a two-year term.

3. Two appointments for nonattorney members shall be for a three-year term.

4. One appointment for an attorney member shall be for a one-year term.

5. One appointments for an attorney member shall be for a two-year term.

G. The members currently serving on the commission may continue to serve until the expiration of their normal terms. All subsequent appointments shall be made as prescribed by this section.

Section 37. Judicial vacancies and appointments; initial terms; residence; age

A. Within sixty days from the occurrence of a vacancy in the office of a justice or judge of any court of record, except for vacancies occurring in the office of a judge of the superior court or a judge of a court of record inferior to the superior court, the commission on appellate court appointments, if the vacancy is in the supreme court or an intermediate appellate court of record, shall submit to the governor the names of not less than three persons nominated by it to fill such vacancy, no more than two of whom shall be members of the same political party unless there are more than four such nominees, in which event not more than sixty percentum of such nominees shall be members of the same political party.

B. Within sixty days from the occurrence of a vacancy in the office of a judge of the superior court or a judge of a court of record inferior to the superior court except for vacancies occurring in the office of a judge of the superior court or a judge of a court of record inferior to the superior court in a county having a population of less than two hundred fifty thousand persons according to the most recent United States census, the commission on trial court appointments for the county in which the vacancy occurs shall submit to the governor the names of not less than three persons nominated by it to fill such vacancy, no more than two of whom shall be members of the same political party unless there are more than four such nominees, in which event no more than sixty per centum of such nominees shall be members of the same political party. A nominee shall be under sixty-five years of age at the time his name is submitted to the governor. Judges of the superior court shall be subject to retention or rejection by a vote of the qualified electors of the county from which they were appointed at the general election in the manner provided by section 38 of this article.

C. A vacancy in the office of a justice or a judge of such courts of record shall be filled by appointment by the governor without regard to political affiliation from one of the nominees whose names shall be submitted to him as hereinabove provided. In making the appointment, the governor shall consider the diversity of the state's population for an appellate court appointment and the diversity of the county's population for a trial court appointment, however the primary consideration shall be merit. If the governor does not appoint one of such nominees to fill such vacancy within sixty days after their names are submitted to the governor by such commission, the chief justice of the supreme court forthwith shall appoint on the basis of merit alone without regard to political affiliation one of such nominees to fill such vacancy. If such commission does not, within sixty days after such vacancy occurs, submit the names of nominees as hereinabove provided, the governor shall have the power to appoint any qualified person to fill such vacancy at any time thereafter prior to the time the names of the nominees to fill such vacancy are submitted to the governor as hereinabove provided. Each justice or judge so appointed shall initially hold office for a term ending sixty days following the next regular general election after the expiration of a term of two years in office. Thereafter, the terms of justices or judges of the supreme court and the superior court shall be as provided by this article.

D. A person appointed to fill a vacancy on an intermediate appellate court or another court of record now existing or hereafter established by law shall have been a resident of the counties or county in which that vacancy exists for at least one year prior to his appointment, in addition to possessing the other required qualifications. A nominee shall be under sixty-five years of age at the time his name is submitted to the governor.

Section 38. Declaration of candidacy; form of judicial ballot, rejection and retention; failure to file declaration

A. A justice or judge of the supreme court or an intermediate appellate court shall file in the office of the secretary of state, and a judge of the superior court or other court of record including such justices or judges who are holding office as such by election or appointment at the time of the adoption of this section except for judges of the superior court and other courts of record inferior to the superior court in counties having a population of less than two hundred fifty thousand persons, according to the United States census, shall file in the office of the clerk of the board of supervisors of the county in which he regularly sits and resides, not less than sixty nor more than ninety days prior to the regular general election next preceding the expiration of his term of office, a declaration of his desire to be retained in office, and the secretary of state shall certify to the several boards of supervisors the appropriate names of the candidate or candidates appearing on such declarations filed in his office.

B. The name of any justice or judge whose declaration is filed as provided in this section shall be placed on the appropriate official ballot at the next regular general election under a nonpartisan designation and in substantially the following form:

Shall _____, (Name of justice or judge) of the _____ court be retained in office? Yes __ No __ (Mark X after one).

C. If a majority of those voting on the question votes "No," then, upon the expiration of the term for which such justice or judge was serving, a vacancy shall exist, which shall be filled as provided by this article. If a majority of those voting on the question votes "Yes," such justice or judge shall remain in office for another term, subject to removal as provided by this constitution.

D. The votes shall be counted and canvassed and the result declared as in the case of state and county elections, whereupon a certificate of retention or rejection of the incumbent justice or judge shall be delivered to him by the secretary of state or the clerk of the board of supervisors, as the case may be.

E. If a justice or judge fails to file a declaration of his desire to be retained in office, as required by this section, then his office shall become vacant upon expiration of the term for which such justice or judge was serving.

Section 39. Retirement of justices and judges; vacancies

On attaining the age of seventy years a justice or judge of a court of record shall retire and his judicial office shall be vacant, except as otherwise provided in section 35 of this article. In addition to becoming vacant as provided in this section, the office of a justice or judge of any court of record becomes vacant upon his death or his voluntary retirement pursuant to statute or his voluntary resignation, and also, as provided in section 38 of this article, upon the expiration of his term next following a general election at which a majority of those voting on the question of his retention vote in the negative or for which general election he is required, but fails, to file a declaration of his desire to be retained in office.

This section is alternative to and cumulative with the methods of removal of judges and justices provided in parts 1 and 2 of article VIII and article 6.1 of this Constitution.

Section 40. Option for counties with less than two hundred fifty thousand persons

Notwithstanding any provision of this article to the contrary, any county having a population of less than two hundred fifty thousand persons, according to the most recent United States census, may choose to select its judges of the superior court or of courts of record inferior to the superior court as if it had a population of two hundred fifty thousand or more persons. Such choice shall be determined by vote of the qualified electors of such county voting on the question at an election called for such purpose by resolution of the board of supervisors of such county. If such qualified electors approve, the provisions of sections 12, 28, 30, 35 through 39, 41 and 42 shall apply as if such county had a population of two hundred fifty thousand persons or more.

Section 41. Superior court divisions; commission on trial court appointments; membership; terms

A. Except as otherwise provided, judges of the superior court in counties having a population of two hundred fifty thousand persons or more according to the most recent United States census shall hold office for a regular term of four years.

B. There shall be a nonpartisan commission on trial court appointments for each county having a population of two hundred fifty thousand persons or more according to the most recent United States census which shall be composed of the following members:

1. The chief justice of the supreme court, who shall be the chairman of the commission. In the event of the absence or incapacity of the chairman the supreme court shall appoint a justice thereof to serve in his place and stead.

2. Five attorney members, none of whom shall reside in the same supervisorial district and not more than three of whom shall be members of the same political party, who are nominated by the board of governors of the state bar of Arizona and who are appointed by the governor subject to confirmation by the senate in the manner prescribed by law.

3. Ten nonattorney members, no more than two of whom shall reside in the same supervisorial district.

C. At least ninety days prior to a term expiring or within twenty-one days of a vacancy occurring for a nonattorney member on the commission for trial court appointments, the member of the board of supervisors from the district in which the vacancy has occurred shall appoint a nominating committee of seven members who reside in the district, not more than four of whom may be from the same political party. The make-up of the committee shall, to the extent feasible, reflect the diversity of the population of the district. Members shall not be attorneys and shall not hold any governmental office, elective or appointive, for profit. The committee shall provide public notice that a vacancy exists and shall solicit, review and forward to the governor all applications along with the committee's recommendations for appointment. The governor shall appoint two persons from each supervisorial district who shall not be of the same political party, subject to confirmation by the senate in the manner prescribed by law.

D. In making or confirming appointments to trial court commissions, the governor, the senate and the state bar shall endeavor to see that the commission reflects the diversity of the county's population.

E. Members of the commission shall serve staggered four year terms, except that initial appointments for the five additional nonattorney members and the two additional attorney members of the commission shall be designated by the governor as follows:

1. One appointment for a nonattorney member shall be for a one-year term.

2. Two appointments for nonattorney members shall be for a two-year term.

3. Two appointments for nonattorney members shall be for a three-year term.

4. One appointment for an attorney member shall be for a one-year term.

5. One appointment for an attorney member shall be for a two-year term.

F. Vacancies shall be filled for the unexpired terms in the same manner as the original appointments.

G. Attorney members of the commission shall have resided in this state and shall have been admitted to practice in this state by the supreme court for at least five years and shall have resided in the supervisorial district from which they are appointed for at least one year. Nonattorney members shall have resided in this state for at least five years, shall have resided in the supervisorial district for at least one year before being nominated and shall not be judges, retired judges nor admitted to practice before the supreme court. None of the attorney or nonattorney members of the commission shall hold any governmental office, elective or appointive, for profit and no attorney member is eligible for appointment to any judicial office of this state until one year after membership in the commission terminates.

H. No person other than the chief justice shall serve at the same time as a member of more than one judicial appointment commission.

I. The commission shall submit the names of not less than three individuals for nomination for the office of the superior court judge pursuant to section 37 of this article.

J. Prior to making recommendations to the governor, the commission shall conduct investigations, hold public hearings and take public testimony. An executive session as prescribed by rule may be held upon a two-thirds vote of the members of the commission in a public hearing. Final decisions as to recommendations shall be made without regard to political affiliation in an impartial and objective manner. The commission shall consider the diversity of the county's population and the geographical distribution of the residences of the judges throughout the county, however the primary consideration shall be merit. Voting shall be in a public hearing. The expenses of meetings of the commission and the attendance of members thereof for travel and subsistence shall be paid from the general fund of the state as state officers are paid, upon claims approved by the chairman.

K. After public hearings the supreme court shall adopt rules of procedure for the commission on trial court appointments.

L. The members of the commission who were appointed pursuant to section 36 of this article prior to the effective date of this section may continue to serve until the expiration of their normal terms. All subsequent appointments shall be made as prescribed by this section.

Section 42. Retention evaluation of justices and judges

The supreme court shall adopt, after public hearings, and administer for all justices and judges who file a declaration to be retained in office, a process, established by court rules for evaluating judicial performance. The rules shall include written performance standards and performance reviews which survey opinions of persons who have knowledge of the justice's or judge's performance. The public shall be afforded a full and fair opportunity for participation in the evaluation process through public hearings, dissemination of evaluation reports to voters and any other methods as the court deems advisable.

Article 6.1: Commission on Judicial Conduct

Section 1. Composition; appointment; term; vacancies

A. A commission on judicial conduct is created to be composed of eleven persons consisting of two judges of the court of appeals, two judges of the superior court, one justice of the peace and one municipal court judge, who shall be appointed by the supreme court, two members of the state bar of Arizona, who shall be appointed by the governing body of such bar association, and three citizens who are not judges, retired judges nor members of the state bar of Arizona, who shall be appointed by the governor subject to confirmation by the senate in the manner prescribed by law.

B. Terms of members of the commission shall be six years, except that initial terms of two members appointed by the supreme court and one member appointed by the state bar of Arizona for terms which begin in January, 1991 shall be for two years and initial terms of one member appointed by the supreme court and one member appointed by the state bar of Arizona for terms which begin in January, 1991 shall be for four years. If a member ceases to hold the position that qualified him for appointment his membership on the commission terminates. An appointment to fill a vacancy for an unexpired term shall be made for the remainder of the term by the appointing power of the original appointment.

Section 2. Disqualification of judge

A judge is disqualified from acting as a judge, without loss of salary, while there is pending an indictment or an information charging him in the United States with a crime punishable as a felony under Arizona or federal law, or a recommendation to the supreme court by the commission on judicial conduct for his suspension, removal or retirement.

Section 3. Suspension or removal of judge

On recommendation of the commission on judicial conduct, or on its own motion, the supreme court may suspend a judge from office without salary when, in the United States, he pleads guilty or no contest or is found guilty of a crime punishable as a felony under Arizona or federal law or of any other crime that involves moral turpitude under such law. If his conviction is reversed the suspension terminates, and he shall be paid his salary for the period of suspension. If he is suspended and his conviction becomes final the supreme court shall remove him from office.

Section 4. Retirement of judge

A. On recommendation of the commission on judicial conduct, the supreme court may retire a judge for disability that seriously interferes with the performance of his duties and is or is likely to become permanent, and may censure, suspend without pay or remove a judge for action by him that constitutes wilful misconduct in office, wilful and persistent failure to perform his duties, habitual intemperance or conduct prejudicial to the administration of justice that brings the judicial office into disrepute.

B. A judge retired by the supreme court shall be considered to have retired voluntarily. A judge removed by the supreme court is ineligible for judicial office in this state.

Section 5. Definitions and rules implementing article

The term "judge" as used in this article shall apply to all justices of the peace, judges in courts inferior to the superior court as may be provided by law, judges of the superior court, judges of the court of appeals and justices of the supreme court. The supreme court shall make rules implementing this article and providing for confidentiality of proceedings. A judge who is a member of the commission or supreme court shall not participate as a member in any proceedings hereunder involving his own censure, suspension, removal or involuntary retirement.

Section 6. Article self-executing

The provisions of this article shall be self- executing.

Article VII: Suffrage and Elections

Section 1. Method of voting; secrecy

All elections by the people shall be by ballot, or by such other method as may be prescribed by law; Provided, that secrecy in voting shall be preserved.

Section 2. Qualifications of voters; disqualification

A. No person shall be entitled to vote at any general election, or for any office that now is, or hereafter may be, elective by the people, or upon any question which may be submitted to a vote of the people, unless such person be a citizen of the United States of the age of eighteen years or over, and shall have resided in the state for the period of time preceding such election as prescribed by law, provided that qualifications for voters at a general election for the purpose of electing presidential electors shall be as prescribed by law. The word "citizen" shall include persons of the male and female sex.

B. The rights of citizens of the United States to vote and hold office shall not be denied or abridged by the state, or any political division or municipality thereof, on account of sex, and the right to register, to vote and to hold office under any law now in effect, or which may hereafter be enacted, is hereby extended to, and conferred upon males and females alike.

C. No person who is adjudicated an incapacitated person shall be qualified to vote at any election, nor shall any person convicted of treason or felony, be qualified to vote at any election unless restored to civil rights.

Section 3. Voting residence of federal employees and certain others

For the purpose of voting, no person shall be deemed to have gained or lost a residence by reason of being present or absent while employed in the service of the United States, or while a student at any institution of learning, or while kept at any institution or other shelter at public expense, or while confined in any public jail or prison.

Section 4. Privilege of electors from arrest

Electors shall in all cases, except treason, felony, or breach of the peace, be privileged from arrest during their attendance at any election, and in going thereto and returning therefrom.

Section 5. Military duty on day of election

No elector shall be obliged to perform military duty on the day of an election, except in time of war or public danger.

Section 6. Residence of military personnel stationed within state

No soldier, seaman, or marine, in the army or navy of the United States shall be deemed a resident of this state in consequence of his being stationed at any military or naval place within this state.

Section 7. Highest number of votes received as determinative of person elected

In all elections held by the people in this state, the person, or persons, receiving the highest number of legal votes shall be declared elected.

Section 8. Qualifications for voters at school elections

Qualifications for voters at school elections shall be as are now, or as may hereafter be, provided by law.

Section 9. Advisory vote

For the purpose of obtaining an advisory vote of the people, the legislature shall provide for placing the names of candidates for United States senator on the official ballot at the general election next preceding the election of a United States senator.

Section 10. Direct primary election law

The Legislature shall enact a direct primary election law, which shall provide for the nomination of candidates for all elective State, county, and city offices, including candidates for United States Senator and for Representative in Congress. Any person who is registered as no party preference or independent as the party preference or who is registered with a political party that is not qualified for representation on the ballot may vote in the primary election of any one of the political parties that is qualified for the ballot.

Section 11. General elections; date

There shall be a general election of representatives in congress, and of state, county, and precinct officers on the first Tuesday after the first Monday in November of the first even numbered year after the year in which Arizona is admitted to statehood and biennially thereafter.

Section 12. Registration and other laws

There shall be enacted registration and other laws to secure the purity of elections and guard against abuses of the elective franchise.

Section 13. Submission of questions upon bond issues or special assessments

Questions upon bond issues or special assessments shall be submitted to the vote of real property tax payers, who shall also in all respects be qualified electors of this state, and of the political subdivisions thereof affected by such question.

Section 14. Fee for placing candidate's name on ballot

No fee shall ever be required in order to have the name of any candidate placed on the official ballot for any election or primary.

Section 15. Qualifications for public office

Every person elected or appointed to any elective office of trust or profit under the authority of the state, or any political division or any municipality thereof, shall be a qualified elector of the political division or municipality in which such person shall be elected.

Section 16. Campaign contributions and expenditures; publicity

The legislature, at its first session, shall enact a law providing for a general publicity, before and after election, of all campaign contributions to, and expenditures of campaign committees and candidates for public office.

Section 17. Vacancy in Congress

There shall be a primary and general election as prescribed by law, which shall provide for nomination and election of a candidate for United States Senator and for Representative in Congress when a vacancy occurs through resignation or any other cause.

Section 18. Term limits on ballot appearances in congressional elections.

The name of any candidate for United States senator from Arizona shall not appear on the ballot if, by the end of the current term of office, the candidate will have served (or, but for resignation, would have served) in that office for two consecutive terms, and the name of a candidate for United States representative from Arizona shall not appear on the ballot if, by the end of the current term of office, the candidate will have served (or, but for resignation, would have served) in that office for three consecutive terms. Terms are considered consecutive unless they are at least one full term apart. Any person appointed or elected to fill a vacancy in the United States congress who serves at least one half of a term of office shall be considered to have served a term in that office for purposes of this section. For purposes of this section, terms beginning before January 1, 1993 shall not be considered.

Article VIII: Removal From Office

Part 1: Recall of Public Officers

Section 1. Officers subject to recall; petitioners

Every public officer in the state of Arizona, holding an elective office, either by election or appointment, is subject to recall from such office by the qualified electors of the electoral district from which candidates are elected to such office. Such electoral district may include the whole state. Such number of said electors as shall equal twenty-five per centum of the number of votes cast at the last preceding general election for all of the candidates for the office held by such officer, may by petition, which shall be known as a recall petition, demand his recall.

Section 2. Recall petitions; contents; filing; signatures; oath

Every recall petition must contain a general statement, in not more than two hundred words, of the grounds of such demand, and must be filed in the office in which petitions for nominations to the office held by the incumbent are required to be filed. The signatures to such recall petition need not all be on one sheet of paper, but each signer must add to his signature the date of his signing said petition, and his place of residence, giving his street and number, if any, should he reside in a town or city. One of the signers of each sheet of such petition, or the person circulating such sheet, must make and subscribe an oath on said sheet, that the signatures thereon are genuine.

Section 3. Resignation of officer; special election

If such officer shall offer his resignation it shall be accepted, and the vacancy shall be filled as may be provided by law. If he shall not resign within five days after a recall petition is filed as provided by law, a special election shall be ordered to be held as provided by law, to determine whether such officer shall be recalled. On the ballots at such election shall be printed the reasons as set forth in the petition for demanding his recall, and, in not more than two hundred words, the officer's justification of his course in office. He shall continue to perform the duties of his office until the result of such election shall have been officially declared.

Section 4. Special election; candidates; results; qualification of successor

Unless the incumbent otherwise requests, in writing, the incumbent's name shall be placed as a candidate on the official ballot without nomination. Other candidates for the office may be nominated to be voted for at said election. The candidate who receives the highest number of votes shall be declared elected for the remainder of the term. Unless the incumbent receives the highest number of votes, the incumbent shall be deemed to be removed from office, upon qualification of the successor. In the event that the successor shall not qualify within five days after the result of said election shall have been declared, the said office shall be vacant, and may be filled as provided by law.

Section 5. Recall petitions; restrictions and conditions

No recall petition shall be circulated against any officer until he shall have held his office for a period of six months, except that it may be filed against a member of the legislature at any time after five days from the beginning of the first session after his election. After one recall petition and election, no further recall petition shall be filed against the same officer during the term for which he was elected, unless petitioners signing such petition shall first pay into the public treasury which has paid such election expenses, all expenses of the preceding election.

Section 6. Application of general election laws; implementary legislation

The general election laws shall apply to recall elections in so far as applicable. Laws necessary to facilitate the operation of the provisions of this article shall be enacted, including provision for payment by the public treasury of the reasonable special election campaign expenses of such officer.

Part 2: Impeachment

Section 1. Power of impeachment in house of representatives; trial by senate

The house of representatives shall have the sole power of impeachment. The concurrence of a majority of all the members shall be necessary to an impeachment. All impeachments shall be tried by the senate, and, when sitting for that purpose, the senators shall be upon oath or affirmation to do justice according to law and evidence, and shall be presided over by the chief justice of the supreme court. Should the chief justice be on trial, or otherwise disqualified, the senate shall elect a judge of the supreme court to preside.

Section 2. Conviction; grounds for impeachment; judgment; liability to trial

No person shall be convicted without a concurrence of two-thirds of the senators elected. The governor and other state and judicial officers, except justices of courts not of record, shall be liable to impeachment for high crimes, misdemeanors, or malfeasance in office, but judgment in such cases shall extend only to removal from office and disqualification to hold any office of honor, trust, or profit in the state. The party, whether convicted or acquitted, shall, nevertheless, be liable to trial and punishment according to law.

Article IX: Public Debt, Revenue, and Taxation

Section 1. Surrender of power of taxation; uniformity of taxes

The power of taxation shall never be surrendered, suspended or contracted away. Except as provided by section 18 of this article, all taxes shall be uniform upon the same class of property within the territorial limits of the authority levying the tax, and shall be levied and collected for public purposes only.

Section 2. Property subject to taxation; exemptions

(1) There shall be exempt from taxation all federal, state, county and municipal property.

(2) Property of educational, charitable and religious associations or institutions not used or held for profit may be exempt from taxation by law.

(3) Public debts, as evidenced by the bonds of Arizona, its counties, municipalities or other subdivisions, shall also be exempt from taxation.

(4) All household goods owned by the user thereof and used solely for noncommercial purposes shall be exempt from taxation, and such person entitled to such exemption shall not be required to take any affirmative action to receive the benefit of such exemption.

(5) Stocks of raw or finished materials, unassembled parts, work in process or finished products constituting the inventory of a retailer or wholesaler located within the state and principally engaged in the resale of such materials, parts or products, whether or not for resale to the ultimate consumer, shall be exempt from taxation.

(6) The legislature may exempt personal property that is used for agricultural purposes or in a trade or business from taxation in a manner provided by law, except that the exemption does not apply to any amount of the full cash value of the personal property of a taxpayer that exceeds fifty thousand dollars. The legislature may provide by law to increase the exempt amount according to annual variations in a designated national inflation index.

(7) The legislature may exempt the property of cemeteries that are set apart and used to inter deceased human beings from taxation in a manner provided by law.

(8) There shall be further exempt from taxation the property of each honorably discharged airman, soldier, sailor, United States marine, member of revenue marine service, the coast guard, nurse corps or of any predecessor or of the component of auxiliary of any thereof, resident of this state, in the amount of:

(a) One thousand five hundred dollars if the total assessment of such person does not exceed three thousand five hundred dollars.

(b) One thousand dollars if the total assessment of such person does not exceed four thousand dollars.

(c) Five hundred dollars if the total assessment of such person does not exceed four thousand five hundred dollars.

(d) Two hundred fifty dollars if the total assessment of such person does not exceed five thousand dollars.

(e) No exemption if the total assessment of such person exceeds five thousand dollars.

No such exemption shall be made for such person unless such person shall have served at least sixty days in the military or naval service of the United States during World War I or prior wars and shall have been a resident of this state prior to September 1, 1945.

(9) There shall be further exempt from taxation as herein provided the property of each honorably discharged airman, soldier, sailor, United States marine, member of revenue marine service, the coast guard, nurse corps or of any predecessor or of the component of auxiliary of any thereof, resident of this state, where such person has a service-connected disability as determined by the United States veterans administration or its successor. No such exemption shall be made for such person unless he shall have been a resident of this state prior to September 1, 1945 or unless such person shall have been a resident of this state for at least four years prior to his original entry into service as an airman, soldier, sailor, United States marine, member of revenue marine service, the coast guard, nurse corps or of any predecessor or of the component of auxiliary of any thereof. The property of such person having a compensable service-connected disability exempt from taxation as herein provided shall be determined as follows:

(a) If such person's service-connected disability as determined by the United States veterans administration or its successor is sixty per cent or less, the property of such person exempt from taxation shall be determined by such person's percentage of disability multiplied by the assessment of such person in the amount of:

(i) One thousand five hundred dollars if the total assessment of such person does not exceed three thousand five hundred dollars.

(ii) One thousand dollars if the total assessment of such person does not exceed four thousand dollars.

(iii) Five hundred dollars if the total assessment of such person does not exceed four thousand five hundred dollars.

(iv) Two hundred fifty dollars if the total assessment of such person does not exceed five thousand dollars.

(v) No exemption if the total assessment of such person exceeds five thousand dollars.

(b) If such person's service-connected disability as determined by the United States veterans administration or its successor is more than sixty per cent, the property of such person exempt from taxation shall be in the amount of:

(i) One thousand five hundred dollars if the total assessment of such person does not exceed three thousand five hundred dollars.

(ii) One thousand dollars if the total assessment of such person does not exceed four thousand dollars.

(iii) Five hundred dollars if the total assessment of such person does not exceed four thousand five hundred dollars.

(iv) Two hundred fifty dollars if the total assessment of such person does not exceed five thousand dollars.

(v) No exemption if the total assessment of such person exceeds five thousand dollars.

(10) There shall be further exempt from taxation the property of each honorably discharged airman, soldier, sailor, United States marine, member of revenue marine service, the coast guard, nurse corps or of any predecessor or of the component of auxiliary of any thereof, resident of this state, where such person has a nonservice-connected total and permanent disability, physical or mental, as so certified by the United States veterans administration, or its successor, or such other certification as provided by law, in the amount of:

(a) One thousand five hundred dollars if the total assessment of such person does not exceed three thousand five hundred dollars.

(b) One thousand dollars if the total assessment of such person does not exceed four thousand dollars.

(c) Five hundred dollars if the total assessment of such person does not exceed four thousand five hundred dollars.

(d) Two hundred fifty dollars if the total assessment of such person does not exceed five thousand dollars.

(e) No exemption if the total assessment of such person exceeds five thousand dollars.

No such exemption shall be made for such person unless he shall have served at least sixty days in the military or naval service of the United States during time of war after World War I and shall have been a resident of this state prior to September 1, 1945.

(11) There shall be further exempt from taxation the property of each widow, resident of this state, in the amount of:

(a) One thousand five hundred dollars if the total assessment of such widow does not exceed three thousand five hundred dollars.

(b) One thousand dollars if the total assessment of such widow does not exceed four thousand dollars.

(c) Five hundred dollars if the total assessment of such widow does not exceed four thousand five hundred dollars.

(d) Two hundred fifty dollars if the total assessment of such widow does not exceed five thousand dollars.

(e) No exemption if the total assessment of such widow exceeds five thousand dollars.

In order to qualify for this exemption, the income from all sources of such widow, together with the income from all sources of all children of such widow residing with the widow in her residence in the year immediately preceding the year for which such widow applies for this exemption, shall not exceed:

1. Seven thousand dollars if none of the widow's children under the age of eighteen years resided with her in such widow's residence; or

2. Ten thousand dollars if one or more of the widow's children residing with her in such widow's residence was under the age of eighteen years, or was totally and permanently disabled, physically or mentally, as certified by competent medical authority as provided by law.

Such widow shall have resided with her last spouse in this state at the time of the spouse's death if she was not a widow and a resident of this state prior to January 1, 1969.

(12) No property shall be exempt which has been conveyed to evade taxation. The total exemption from taxation granted to the property owned by a person who qualifies for any exemption in accordance with the terms of subsections (8), (9), (10) or (11) shall not exceed one thousand five hundred dollars. The provisions of this section shall be self-executing.

(13) All property in the state not exempt under the laws of the United States or under this constitution or exempt by law under the provisions of this section shall be subject to taxation to be ascertained as provided by law.

Article X: State and School Lands

Section 1. Acceptance and holding of lands by state in trust

All lands expressly transferred and confirmed to the state by the provisions of the Enabling Act approved June 20, 1910, including all lands granted to the state and all lands heretofore granted to the Territory of Arizona, and all lands otherwise acquired by the state, shall be by the state accepted and held in trust to be disposed of in whole or in part, only in manner as in the said Enabling Act and in this Constitution provided, and for the several objects specified in the respective granting and confirmatory provisions. The natural products and money proceeds of any of said lands shall be subject to the same trusts as the lands producing the same.

Section 2. Unauthorized disposition of land or proceeds as breach of trust

Disposition of any of said lands, or of any money or thing of value directly or indirectly derived therefrom, for any object other than that for which such particular lands (or the lands from which such money or thing of value shall have been derived) were granted or confirmed, or in any manner contrary to the provisions of the said Enabling Act, shall be deemed a breach of trust.

Section 3. Mortgage or other encumbrance; sale or lease at public auction

No mortgage or other encumbrance of the said lands, or any part thereof, shall be valid in favor of any person or for any purpose or under any circumstances whatsoever. Said lands shall not be sold or leased, in whole or in part, except to the highest and best bidder at a public auction to be held at the county seat of the county wherein the lands to be affected, or the major portion thereof, shall lie, notice of which public auction shall first have been duly given by advertisement, which shall set forth the nature, time and place of the transaction to be had, with a full description of the lands to be offered, and be published once each week for not less than ten successive weeks in a newspaper of general circulation published regularly at the state capital, and in that newspaper of like circulation which shall then be regularly published nearest to the location of the lands so offered; nor shall any sale or contract for the sale of any timber or other natural product of such lands be made, save at the place, in the manner, and after the notice by publication provided for sales and leases of the lands themselves. Nothing herein, or elsewhere in article X contained, shall prevent:

1. The leasing of any of the lands referred to in this article in such manner as the legislature may prescribe, for grazing, agricultural, commercial and homesite purposes, for a term of ten years or less, without advertisement;

2. The leasing of any of said lands, in such manner as the legislature may prescribe, whether or not also leased for grazing and agricultural purposes, for mineral purposes, other than for the exploration, development, and production of oil, gas and other hydrocarbon substances, for a term of twenty years or less, without advertisement, or,

3. The leasing of any of said lands, whether or not also leased for other purposes, for the exploration, development, and production of oil, gas and other hydrocarbon substances on, in or under said lands for an initial term of twenty (20) years or less and as long thereafter as oil, gas or other hydrocarbon substance may be procured therefrom in paying quantities, the leases to be made in any manner, with or without advertisement, bidding, or appraisement, and under such terms and provisions, as the legislature may prescribe, the terms and provisions to include a reservation of a royalty to the state of not less than twelve and one-half per cent of production.

Section 4. Sale or other disposal; appraisal; minimum price; credit; passing of title

All lands, lease-holds, timber, and other products of land, before being offered, shall be appraised at their true value, and no sale or other disposal thereof shall be made for a consideration less than the value so ascertained, nor in any case less than the minimum price hereinafter fixed, nor upon credit unless accompanied by ample security, and the legal title shall not be deemed to have passed until the consideration shall have been paid.

Section 5. Minimum price; relinquishment of lands to United States

No lands shall be sold for less than three dollars per acre, and no lands which are or shall be susceptible of irrigation under any projects now or hereafter completed or adopted by the United States under legislation for the reclamation of lands, or under any other project for the reclamation of lands, shall be sold at less than twenty-five dollars per acre; Provided, that the state, at the request of the secretary of the interior, shall from time to time relinquish such of its lands to the United States as at any time are needed for irrigation works in connection with any such government project, and other lands in lieu thereof shall be selected from lands of the character named and in the manner prescribed in section twenty-four of the said Enabling Act.

Section 6. Lands reserved by United States for development of water power

No lands reserved and excepted of the lands granted to this state by the United States, actually or prospectively valuable for the development of water powers or power for hydro-electric use or transmission, which shall be ascertained and designated by the secretary of the interior within five years after the proclamation of the president declaring the admission of the state, shall be subject to any disposition whatsoever by the state or by any officer of the state, and any conveyance or transfer of such lands made within said five years shall be null and void.

Section 7. Establishment of permanent funds; segregation, investment and distribution of monies; exception; resolution of litigation

A. A separate permanent fund shall be established for each of the several objects for which the said grants are made and confirmed by the enabling act to the state, and whenever any monies shall be in any manner derived from any of said lands, the same shall be deposited by the state treasurer in the permanent fund corresponding to the grant under which the particular land producing such monies was, by the enabling act, conveyed or confirmed.

B. No monies shall ever be taken from one permanent fund for deposit in any other, or for any object other than that for which the land producing the same was granted or confirmed.

C. All such monies shall be invested in safe interest-bearing securities and prudent equity securities consistent with the requirements of this section.

D. The legislature shall establish a board of investment to serve as trustees of the permanent funds. The board shall provide for the management of the assets of the funds consistent with the following conditions:

1. Not more than sixty percent of a fund at cost may be invested in equities at any time.

2. Equities that are eligible for purchase are restricted to stocks listed on any national stock exchange or eligible for trading through the United States national association of securities dealers automated quotation system, or successor institutions, except as may be prohibited by general criteria or by a restriction on investment in a specific security adopted pursuant to this subsection.

3. Not more than five percent of all of the funds combined at cost may be invested in equity securities issued by the same institution, agency or corporation, other than securities issued as direct obligations of and fully guaranteed by the United States government.

E. In making investments under this section the state treasurer and trustees shall exercise the judgment and care under the prevailing circumstances that an institutional investor of ordinary prudence, discretion and intelligence exercises in managing large investments entrusted to it, not in regard to speculation, but in regard to the permanent disposition of monies, considering the probable safety of capital as well as the probable total rate of return over extended periods of time.

F. The earnings, interest, dividends and realized capital gains and losses from investment of a permanent fund, shall be credited to that fund.

G. The board of investment shall determine the amount of the annual distributions required by this section and allocate distributions pursuant to law. The annual distribution from the permanent funds:

1. For fiscal years 2012-2013 through 2014-2015, shall be two and one-half percent of the average monthly market values of the fund for the immediately preceding five calendar years.

2. For fiscal years 2015-2016 through 2024-2025, shall be six and nine-tenths percent of the average monthly market values of the fund for the immediately preceding five calendar years, except that in fiscal year 2015-2016, the distribution made from the permanent state school fund shall be $259,266,200.

3. Beginning with fiscal year 2025-2026, shall be two and one-half percent of the average monthly market values of the fund for the immediately preceding five calendar years.

H. For fiscal years 2015-2016 through 2024-2025, any increase in expendable earnings under section 37-521, subsection B, paragraph 4, Arizona Revised Statutes, that results from a distribution of more than two and one-half percent of the average monthly market values of the fund for the immediately preceding five calendar years pursuant to subsection G, paragraph 2 of this section shall be appropriated for basic state aid, including inflation adjustments required by section 15-901.01, Arizona Revised Statutes.

I. On or before February 1 of each year, if the average monthly market values of the fund for the immediately preceding five calendar years have decreased compared to the average monthly market values of the fund for the five-calendar-year period that immediately precedes the preceding five calendar years, the director of the office of strategic planning and budgeting, or its successor agency, and the director of the joint legislative budget committee, or its successor agency, shall jointly notify the governor, the president of the senate and the speaker of the house of representatives that a reduction to the distribution prescribed in subsection G, paragraph 2 of this section is necessary to preserve the safety of the capital in the fund. On receipt of that notification, the legislature may enact legislation, with the approval of the governor, that reduces the distribution in subsection G, paragraph 2 of this section for the next fiscal year to at least two and one-half percent but less than six and nine-tenths percent of the average monthly market values of the fund for the immediately preceding five calendar years.

J. Any amount reduced pursuant to subsection I of this section is not required to be paid or distributed:

1. From any other source of public monies.

2. In any subsequent fiscal year.

K. If the legislature enacts legislation, with the approval of the governor, that reduces the distribution pursuant to subsection I of this section:

1. The legislature may reduce the base level for the next fiscal year by an amount commensurate with the reduction in the distribution from the permanent state school fund for the next fiscal year.

2. The amounts from the base level reduction are not required to be paid or distributed in any subsequent fiscal year.

3. The base level reduction is not part of the calculation of the base level for subsequent fiscal years.

L. This section preserves the authority vested in the legislature pursuant to this constitution.

M. This section and article XI, section 11 of this Constitution and the terms and appropriations of house bill 2001, fifty second legislature, first special session, fully satisfy the requirements of section 15-901.01, Arizona Revised Statutes.

Section 8. Conformity of contracts with enabling act

Every sale, lease, conveyance, or contract of or concerning any of the lands granted or confirmed, or the use thereof or the natural products thereof made to this state by the said Enabling Act, not made in substantial conformity with the provisions thereof, shall be null and void.

Section 9. Sale or lease; conditions; limitations; lease prior to adoption of constitution

All lands expressly transferred and confirmed to the state, by the provisions of the Enabling Act approved June 20, 1910, including all lands granted to the state, and all lands heretofore granted to the territory of Arizona, and all lands otherwise acquired by the state, may be sold or leased by the state in the manner, and on the conditions, and with the limitations, prescribed by the said Enabling Act and this Constitution, and as may be further prescribed by law; Provided, that the legislature shall provide for the separate appraisement of the lands and of the improvements on school and university lands which have been held under lease prior to the adoption of this Constitution, and for reimbursement to the actual bona fide residents or lessees of such lands upon which such improvements are situated, as prescribed by title 65, Civil Code of Arizona, 1901, and in such cases only as permit reimbursements to lessees in said title 65.

Section 10. Laws for sale or lease of state lands; protection of residents and lessees

The legislature shall provide by proper laws for the sale of all state lands or the lease of such lands, and shall further provide by said laws for the protection of the actual bona fide residents and lessees of said lands, whereby such residents and lessees of said lands shall be protected in their rights to their improvements (including water rights) in such manner that in case of lease to other parties the former lessee shall be paid by the succeeding lessee the value of such improvements and rights and actual bona fide residents and lessees shall have preference to a renewal of their leases at a reassessed rental to be fixed as provided by law.

Section 11. Maximum acreage allowed single purchaser

No individual, corporation or association shall be allowed to purchase more than one hundred sixty (160) acres of agricultural land or more than six hundred forty (640) acres of grazing land.

Section 12. Land exchanges; purposes; notice; hearings; submission to the voters

A. The legislature shall provide a process by law for exchanging lands granted or confirmed by the enabling act for public lands in this state under the terms and conditions prescribed by this section.

B. The purpose of the exchange must be either:

1. To assist in preserving and protecting military facilities in this state from encroaching development.

2. To improve the management of state lands for the purpose of sale or lease or conversion to public use of state lands.

C. Before the public hearings are held pursuant to subsection D, paragraph 3 of this section:

1. At least two independent appraisals must be made available to the public showing that the true value of any lands the state receives in the exchange equals or exceeds the true value of the lands the state conveys.

2. At least two independent analyses of the proposed exchange must be made available to the public showing:

(a) The income to the trust before the exchange from all lands the state conveys and the projected income to the trust after the exchange from all lands the state receives.

(b) The fiscal impact of the exchange on each county, city, town and school district in which all the lands involved in the exchange are located.

(c) The physical, economic and natural resource impacts of the proposed exchange on the surrounding or directly adjacent local community and the impacts on local land uses and land use plans.

D. Land may not be exchanged unless:

1. The exchange is in the best interest of the state land trust.

2. Public notice of the proposed exchange includes full disclosure of all details of the transaction, the ownership of all parcels of the lands involved in the exchange, including independent and ancillary parties, a legal and general description of the location of all parcels of the lands and the appraised value of all parcels of the lands.

3. Public hearings are held at the state capital and in a location of general accessibility in the vicinity of the state lands being exchanged. Notice of the time and place of the hearings must be given beginning at least six weeks before each hearing in a manner prescribed by law. During this period, a process shall be provided for public comment on the proposed exchange.

4. The exchange is approved by the qualified electors of this state in the manner of a referendum pursuant to article IV, part 1, section 1 at the next regular general election. To be approved, the proposition must receive an affirmative vote of a majority of the qualified electors voting on the measure.

E. Land exchanges are not considered to be sales for the purposes of this article.

Article XI: Education

Section 1. Public school system; education of pupils who are hearing and vision impaired

A. The legislature shall enact such laws as shall provide for the establishment and maintenance of a general and uniform public school system, which system shall include:

1. Kindergarten schools.

2. Common schools.

3. High schools.

4. Normal schools.

5. Industrial schools.

6. Universities, which shall include an agricultural college, a school of mines, and such other technical schools as may be essential, until such time as it may be deemed advisable to establish separate state institutions of such character.

B. The legislature shall also enact such laws as shall provide for the education and care of pupils who are hearing and vision impaired.

Section 2. Conduct and supervision of school system

The general conduct and supervision of the public school system shall be vested in a state board of education, a state superintendent of public instruction, county school superintendents, and such governing boards for the state institutions as may be provided by law.

Section 3. State board of education; composition; powers and duties; compensation

The state board of education shall be composed of the following members: the superintendent of public instruction, the president of a state university or a state college, four lay members, a president or chancellor of a community college district, a person who is an owner or administrator of a charter school, a superintendent of a high school district, a classroom teacher and a county school superintendent. Each member, other than the superintendent of public instruction, shall be appointed by the governor with the consent of the senate in the manner prescribed by law. The powers, duties, compensation and expenses, and the terms of office, of the board shall be such as may be prescribed by law.

Section 4. State superintendent of public instruction; board membership; powers and duties

The state superintendent of public instruction shall be a member, and secretary, of the state board of education, and, ex-officio, a member of any other board having control of public instruction in any state institution. His powers and duties shall be prescribed by law.

Section 5. Regents of university and other governing boards; appointments by governor; membership of governor on board of regents

The regents of the university, and the governing boards of other state educational institutions, shall be appointed by the governor with the consent of the senate in the manner prescribed by law, except that the governor shall be, ex-officio, a member of the board of regents of the university.

Section 6. Admission of students of both sexes to state educational institutions; tuition; common school system

The university and all other state educational institutions shall be open to students of both sexes, and the instruction furnished shall be as nearly free as possible. The legislature shall provide for a system of common schools by which a free school shall be established and maintained in every school district for at least six months in each year, which school shall be open to all pupils between the ages of six and twenty-one years.

Section 7. Sectarian instruction; religious or political test or qualification

No sectarian instruction shall be imparted in any school or state educational institution that may be established under this Constitution, and no religious or political test or qualification shall ever be required as a condition of admission into any public educational institution of the state, as teacher, student, or pupil; but the liberty of conscience hereby secured shall not be so construed as to justify practices or conduct inconsistent with the good order, peace, morality, or safety of the state, or with the rights of others.

Section 8. Permanent state school fund; source; apportionment of state funds

A. A permanent state school fund for the use of the common schools shall be derived from the sale of public school lands or other public lands specified in the enabling act approved June 20, 1910; from all estates or distributive shares of estates that may escheat to the state; from all unclaimed shares and dividends of any corporation incorporated under the laws of Arizona; and from all gifts, devises, or bequests made to the state for general educational purposes.

B. The rental derived from school lands, with such other funds as may be provided by law shall be apportioned only for common and high school education in Arizona, and in such manner as may be prescribed by law.

Section 9. County school fund; size of fund; free schools

The amount of this apportionment shall become a part of the county school fund, and the legislature shall enact such laws as will provide for increasing the county fund sufficiently to maintain all the public schools of the county for a minimum term of six months in every school year. The laws of the state shall enable cities and towns to maintain free high schools, industrial schools, and commercial schools.

Section 10. Source of revenue for maintenance of state educational institutions

The revenue for the maintenance of the respective state educational institutions shall be derived from the investment of the proceeds of the sale, and from the rental of such lands as have been set aside by the enabling act approved June 20, 1910, or other legislative enactment of the United States, for the use and benefit of the respective state educational institutions. In addition to such income the legislature shall make such appropriations, to be met by taxation, as shall insure the proper maintenance of all state educational institutions, and shall make such special appropriations as shall provide for their development and improvement.

Section 11. Schools; inflation adjustments; exceptions; definitions

A. On or before February 1 of each year, if the state transaction privilege tax growth rate and the total nonfarm employment growth rate are each at least one percent, but less than two percent, the director of the office of strategic planning and budgeting, or its successor agency, and the director of the joint legislative budget committee, or its successor agency, shall jointly notify the governor, the president of the senate and the speaker of the house of representatives. On receipt of the notification, the legislature is not required to make the inflation adjustments required by section 15-901.01, Arizona Revised Statutes, for the next fiscal year.

B. On or before February 1 of each year, if the state transaction privilege tax growth rate and the total nonfarm employment growth rate are each less than one percent, the director of the office of strategic planning and budgeting, or its successor agency, and the director of the joint legislative budget committee, or its successor agency, shall jointly notify the governor, the president of the senate and the speaker of the house of representatives. On receipt of the notification, the legislature shall not make the inflation adjustments required by section 15-901.01, Arizona Revised Statutes, for the next fiscal year.

C. Beginning in fiscal year 2024-2025, on or before February 1 of each year, if the total amount of general fund appropriations for the Arizona department of education, or its successor agency, is at least forty-nine percent but less than fifty percent of the total general fund appropriation for the current fiscal year, the director of the office of strategic planning and budgeting, or its successor agency, and the director of the joint legislative budget committee, or its successor agency, shall jointly notify the governor, the president of the senate and the speaker of the house of representatives. On receipt of the notification, the legislature:

1. Is not required to make the inflation adjustments required by section 15-901.01, Arizona Revised Statutes, for the next fiscal year.

2. May reduce the base level for the next fiscal year by the amount of the inflation adjustments required by section 15-901.01, Arizona Revised Statutes, made for the current fiscal year.

D. Beginning in fiscal year 2024-2025, on or before February 1 of each year, if the total amount of general fund appropriations for the Arizona department of education, or its successor agency, is at least fifty percent of the total general fund appropriation for the current fiscal year, the director of the office of strategic planning and budgeting, or its successor agency, and the director of the joint legislative budget committee, or its successor agency, shall jointly notify the governor, the president of the senate and the speaker of the house of representatives. On receipt of the notification, the legislature:

1. Is not required to make the inflation adjustments required by section 15-901.01, Arizona Revised Statutes, for the next fiscal year.

2. May reduce the base level for the next fiscal year by two times the amount of the inflation adjustments required by section 15-901.01, Arizona Revised Statutes, made for the current fiscal year.

E. If the inflation adjustments required by section 15-901.01, Arizona Revised Statutes, are not required to be made or are prohibited from being made pursuant to this section for a fiscal year, the omitted inflation adjustment amounts:

1. Are not required to be paid or distributed in any subsequent fiscal year.

2. Become a part of the calculation of the base level for subsequent fiscal years.

F. If base level reductions are made pursuant to subsection C or D of this section for a fiscal year, the reduced amounts:

1. Are not required to be paid or distributed in any subsequent fiscal year.

2. Do not become part of the calculation of the base level for subsequent fiscal years.

G. This section preserves the authority vested in the legislature pursuant to this constitution.

H. For the purposes of this section:

1. "Total nonfarm employment growth rate" means the percentage change in the seasonally adjusted total nonfarm employment in this state from the final month of the most recent calendar year to the final month of the immediately preceding calendar year, as reported by the Arizona department of administration or its successor agency.

2. "State transaction privilege tax growth rate" means the percentage change in the revenues derived from the state transaction privilege tax that are distributed to the state general fund from the most recent calendar year to the immediately preceding calendar year, as reported by the Arizona department of revenue or its successor agency.

Article XII: Counties

Section 1. Counties as bodies politic and corporate

Each county of the state, now or hereafter organized, shall be a body politic and corporate.

Section 2. Counties of territory as counties of state

The several counties of the territory of Arizona as fixed by statute at the time of the adoption of this Constitution are hereby declared to be the counties of the state until changed by law.

Section 3. County officers; election; term of office

There are hereby created in and for each organized county of the state the following officers who shall be elected by the qualified electors thereof: a sheriff, a county attorney, a recorder, a treasurer, an assessor, a superintendent of schools and at least three supervisors, each of whom shall be elected and hold his office for a term of four (4) years beginning on the first of January next after his election, which number of supervisors is subject to increase by law. The supervisors shall be nominated and elected from districts as provided by law.

The candidates for these offices elected in the general election of November 3, 1964 shall take office on the first day of January, 1965 and shall serve until the first day of January, 1969.

Section 4. County officers; duties, powers, and qualifications; salaries

The duties, powers, and qualifications of such officers shall be as prescribed by law. The board of supervisors of each county is hereby empowered to fix salaries for all county and precinct officers within such county for whom no compensation is provided by law, and the salaries so fixed shall remain in full force and effect until changed by general law.

Section 5. Charter committee; charter preparation; approval

A. The board of supervisors of any county with a population of more than five hundred thousand persons as determined by the most recent United States decennial or special census may call for an election to cause a charter committee to be elected by the qualified electors of that county at any time. Alternatively, the board of supervisors of any county with a population of more than five hundred thousand persons as determined by the most recent United States decennial or special census shall call for the election of the charter committee within ten days after receipt by the clerk of the board of supervisors of a petition that demands the election and that is signed by a number of qualified electors of the county at least equal to ten per cent of the total number of ballots cast for all candidates for governor or presidential electors in the county at the last preceding general election. The election shall be held at least one hundred days but not more than one hundred twenty days after the call for the election. Except as otherwise provided in this section, for elections held under this section or section 6 of this article, the manner of conducting and voting at an election, contesting an election, canvassing votes and certifying returns shall be the same, as nearly as practicable, as in elections for county officers.

B. At the election a vote shall be taken to elect members of the charter committee who will function if further proceedings are authorized and the ballot shall contain the question of whether further proceedings toward adopting a charter shall be authorized pursuant to the call for the election. Unless a majority of the qualified electors voting on the question votes to authorize further proceedings, the election of members of the charter committee shall be invalidated and no further proceedings may be had except pursuant to a subsequent call pursuant to subsection A.

C. The charter committee shall be composed of fifteen qualified electors of the county elected by supervisorial district with the same number serving from each district. A nomination petition for election to the charter committee shall be made available by the clerk of the board of supervisors and shall be signed by a number of qualified electors of the supervisorial district who are eligible to vote for the nominee at least equal to one per cent of the total number of ballots cast for all candidates for governor or presidential electors in the supervisorial district at the last preceding general election, and filed with the clerk not later than sixty days before the election. All qualified electors of the county, including all elected public officials, are eligible to seek election to the charter committee.

D. Within one hundred eighty days after the election the charter committee shall prepare and submit a proposed charter for the county. The proposed charter shall be signed by a majority of the members of the committee and filed with the clerk of the board of supervisors, after which the charter committee shall be dissolved. The county shall then publish the proposed charter in the official newspaper of the county at least once a week for three consecutive weeks. The first publication shall be made within twenty days after the proposed charter is filed with the clerk of the board of supervisors.

E. At least forty-five days but not more than sixty days after final publication, the proposed charter shall be submitted to the vote of the qualified electors of the county at a general or special election. If a general election will be held within ninety days after final publication, the charter shall be submitted at that general election. The full text of the proposed charter shall be printed in a publicity pamphlet and mailed to each household containing a registered voter at least eleven days before the charter election and the ballot may contain only a summary of the proposed charter provisions. The ballot shall contain a question regarding approval of the proposed charter and the questions pertaining to taxation authority and appointment of officers, if any, provided for in sections 7 and 8 of this article.

F. If a majority of the qualified electors voting ratifies the proposed charter, a copy of the charter, together with a statement setting forth the submission of the charter to the qualified electors and its ratification by them, shall be certified by the clerk of the board of supervisors and shall be submitted to the governor for approval. The governor shall approve the charter within thirty days after its submission if it is not in conflict with, or states that in the event of a conflict is subject to, this constitution and the laws of this state. On approval, the charter becomes the organic law of the county, and certified copies of the charter shall be filed in the office of the secretary of state and with the clerk of the board of supervisors after being recorded in the office of the county recorder. Thereafter all courts shall take judicial notice of the charter.

Section 6. Amendment of charter

A charter shall set forth procedures for amendment of the charter. Proposed amendments shall be submitted to the qualified electors of the county at a general or special election and become effective if ratified by a majority of the qualified electors voting on the amendments and approved by the governor in the manner provided for in section 5 of this article.

Section 7. County charter provisions

A. Charter counties continue to be political subdivisions of this state that exist to aid in the administration of this state's laws and for purposes of self-government. Except as otherwise provided in this article the powers of the legislature over counties are not affected by this section and sections 5, 6, 8 and 9 of this article. Charter counties shall provide the same state mandated services and perform the same state mandated functions as non-charter counties. Charter counties may exercise, if provided by the charter, all powers over local concerns of the county consistent with, and subject to, the constitution and the laws of this state. In matters of strictly local municipal concern, charters adopted pursuant to article XIII shall control in any case of conflict with a county charter adopted pursuant to this article.

B. If a county has framed and adopted a charter and the charter is approved by the governor as provided in this article, the county shall be governed by the terms of its charter and ordinances passed pursuant to its charter. If the charter has been framed, adopted and approved and any of its provisions are in conflict with any county ordinance, rule or regulation relating to local concerns of the counties in force at the time of the adoption and approval of the charter, the provisions of the charter prevail notwithstanding the conflict and operate as a repeal or suspension of the law to the extent of conflict, and the law is not thereafter operative as to such conflict.

C. Notwithstanding article IX, section 1, if proposed and approved in the charter, a charter county may levy and collect:

1. Taxes on a countywide basis to provide services on a countywide basis.

2. Taxes on a specially designated area basis to provide services or special levels of service to that area.

All taxes levied pursuant to this subsection shall be uniform upon the same class of property within the territorial limits of the county or the specially designated area and shall be levied and collected for public purposes only.

D. The decision to include a charter provision authorizing taxation pursuant to subsection C, paragraph 1 or 2 of this section shall be placed on the ballot as separate questions at the election to ratify the charter and must be approved by a majority of the qualified electors voting at the election. The result of the voting on either provision authorizing taxation does not affect the result of the voting to ratify the charter. Charter provisions authorizing taxation pursuant to subsection C, paragraph 1 or 2 of this section may also be proposed by an amendment to the charter pursuant to section 6 of this article.

E. If the authority to tax pursuant to subsection C, paragraph 2 of this section is approved for inclusion in the charter, any new tax proposed by the county under subsection C, paragraph 2 of this section shall be voted on by the qualified electors of the specially designated area. The tax must be ratified by a majority vote of the qualified electors voting at the election.

F. A transaction privilege tax, use tax or similar tax levied by a county pursuant to subsection C, paragraph 1 of this section:

1. May be imposed on only those business activities, or on the use, storage or consumption, which are subject to the comparable state transaction privilege tax, use tax or similar tax.

2. Shall provide all exclusion and exemptions provided by, and administrative provisions consistent with, the comparable state transaction privilege tax, use tax or similar tax.

G. All taxes levied under subsection F of this section shall not exceed an aggregate rate of two per cent when combined with existing taxes levied pursuant to title 42, chapter 8.3.

H. If approved in the charter, a charter county may adopt fees and fee schedules for any county products and county service delivery it provides in the conduct of any official business. Notwithstanding any fee schedules or individual charges provided by state law, the governing body of a charter county may adopt an alternate fee schedule or individual charge. Any fee or charge established pursuant to this section shall be attributable to and defray or cover the current or future costs of the product or service delivery for which the fee or charge is assessed.

I. Taxes raised under the authority of this section shall be subject to the provisions of the county property tax and expenditure limitations pursuant to article IX, sections 19 and 20.

Section 8. Government and other powers

A. The county charter shall provide:

1. For an elective governing body and its method of compensation, its powers, duties and responsibilities, its authority to delegate powers, the method of election and removal of members, the terms of office and the manner of filling vacancies in the governing body.

2. For all officers established under section 3 of this article and article VI, section 23, and such additional officers as the charter may provide for, their election or appointment, consolidation or segregation, method of compensation, powers, duties and responsibilities, authority to delegate powers and, if elected, the method of election and removal, terms of office and the manner of filling vacancies in such offices. If the charter provides for the attorney to remain an elective officer of the county, the charter may provide for an appointive office to carry out the civil representation needs of the county, its departments, agencies, boards, commissions, officials and employees. If the elective governing body provided for in the charter does not consist of supervisors, the charter may provide for elimination of the office of supervisor. If the charter provides for the office of supervisor, the number of supervisors shall be not fewer than five or greater than nine. If the charter provides for the appointment or elimination of an officer established under section 3 of this article or article VI, section 23, or for an appointive office to carry out the civil representation needs of the county, those provisions shall include an effective date not earlier than the expiration of the term of office for the officer commencing in January immediately following the first general election at which the officer is elected following approval of the charter by the voters and shall be placed on the ballot as separate questions at the election to ratify the charter and must be approved by a majority of the qualified electors voting at the election. The result of the voting on any provisions authorizing appointment or elimination of officers does not affect the result of the voting to ratify the charter.

3. For the performance of functions required by statute.

4. For a periodic review of the charter provisions to be conducted at least once every ten years from the time of its ratification by the voters and the procedures for the periodic review.

B. The county charter may provide for other elective and appointive offices.

Section 9. Self-executing provision

The provisions of sections 5 through 8 of this article are self-executing, and no further legislation is required to make them effective.

Article XIII: Municipal Corporations

Section 1. Incorporation and organization; classification

Municipal corporations shall not be created by special laws, but the legislature, by general laws, shall provide for the incorporation and organization of cities and towns and for the classification of such cities and towns in proportion to population, subject to the provisions of this article.

Section 2. Charter; preparation and proposal by board of freeholders; ratification and approval; amendment

Any city containing, now or hereafter, a population of more than three thousand five hundred may frame a charter for its own government consistent with, and subject to, the Constitution and the laws of the state, in the following manner: A board of freeholders composed of fourteen qualified electors of said city may be elected at large by the qualified electors thereof, at a general or special election, whose duty it shall be, within ninety days after such election, to prepare and propose a charter for such city. Such proposed charter shall be signed in duplicate by the members of such board, or a majority of them, and filed, one copy of said proposed charter with the chief executive officer of such city and the other with the county recorder of the county in which said city shall be situated. Such proposed charter shall then be published in one or more newspapers published, and of general circulation, within said city for at least twenty-one days if in a daily paper, or in three consecutive issues if in a weekly paper, and the first publication shall be made within twenty days after the completion of the proposed charter. Within thirty days, and not earlier than twenty days, after such publication, said proposed charter shall be submitted to the vote of the qualified electors of said city at a general or special election. If a majority of such qualified electors voting thereon shall ratify such proposed charter, it shall thereupon be submitted to the governor for his approval, and the governor shall approve it if it shall not be in conflict with this Constitution or with the laws of the state. Upon such approval said charter shall become the organic law of such city and supersede any charter then existing (and all amendments thereto), and all ordinances inconsistent with said new charter. A copy of such charter, certified by the chief executive officer, and authenticated by the seal, of such city, together with a statement similarly certified and authenticated setting forth the submission of such charter to the electors and its ratification by them, shall, after the approval of such charter by the governor, be made in duplicate and filed, one copy in the office of the secretary of state and the other in the archives of the city after being recorded in the office of said county recorder. Thereafter all courts shall take judicial notice of said charter.

The charter so ratified may be amended by amendments proposed and submitted by the legislative authority of the city to the qualified electors thereof (or by petition as hereinafter provided), at a general or special election, and ratified by a majority of the qualified electors voting thereon and approved by the governor as herein provided for the approval of the charter.

Section 3. Election of board of freeholders

An election of such board of freeholders may be called at any time by the legislative authority of any such city. Such election shall be called by the chief executive officer of any such city within ten days after there shall have been filed with him a petition demanding such election, signed by a number of qualified electors residing within such city equal to twenty-five per centum of the total number of votes cast at the next preceding general municipal election. Such election shall be held not later than thirty days after the call therefor. At such election a vote shall be taken upon the question whether further proceedings toward adopting a charter shall be had in pursuance to the call, and unless a majority of the qualified electors voting thereon shall vote to proceed further, no further proceedings shall be had, and all proceedings up to the time of said election shall be of no effect.

Section 4. Franchises; approval of electors; term

No municipal corporation shall ever grant, extend, or renew a franchise without the approval of a majority of the qualified electors residing within its corporate limits who shall vote thereon at a general or special election, and the legislative body of any such corporation shall submit any such matter for approval or disapproval to such electors at any general municipal election, or call a special election for such purpose at any time upon thirty days' notice. No franchise shall be granted, extended, or renewed for a longer time than twenty-five years.

Section 5. Right of municipal corporation to engage in business or enterprise

Every municipal corporation within this state shall have the right to engage in any business or enterprise which may be engaged in by a person, firm, or corporation by virtue of a franchise from said municipal corporation.

Section 6. Franchises; restrictions

No grant, extension, or renewal of any franchise or other use of the streets, alleys, or other public grounds, or ways, of any municipality shall divest the state or any of its subdivisions of its or their control and regulation of such use and enjoyment; nor shall the power to regulate charges for public services be surrendered; and no exclusive franchise shall ever be granted.

Section 7. Irrigation and other districts as political subdivisions

Irrigation, power, electrical, agricultural improvement, drainage, and flood control districts, and tax levying public improvement districts, now or hereafter organized pursuant to law, shall be political subdivisions of the state, and vested with all the rights, privileges and benefits, and entitled to the immunities and exemptions granted municipalities and political subdivisions under this constitution or any law of the state or of the United States; but all such districts shall be exempt from the provisions of sections 7 and 8 of article IX of this constitution.

Article XIV: Corporations Other Than Municipal

Section 1. "Corporation" defined; right to sue and suability

The term "corporation," as used in this article, shall be construed to include all associations and joint stock companies having any powers or privileges of corporations not possessed by individuals or co-partnerships, and all corporations shall have the right to sue and shall be subject to be sued, in all courts, in like cases as natural persons.

Section 2. Formation under general laws; change of laws; regulation

Corporations may be formed under general laws, but shall not be created by special acts. Laws relating to corporations may be altered, amended, or repealed at any time, and all corporations doing business in this state may, as to such business, be regulated, limited, and restrained by law.

Section 3. Existing charters

All existing charters under which a bona fide organization shall not have taken place and business commenced in good faith within six months from the time of the approval of this Constitution shall thereafter have no validity.

Section 4. Restriction to business authorized by charter or law

No corporation shall engage in any business other than that expressly authorized in its charter or by the law under which it may have been or may hereafter be organized.

Section 5. Foreign corporations; transaction of business

No corporation organized outside of the limits of this state shall be allowed to transact business within this state on more favorable conditions than are prescribed by law for similar corporations organized under the laws of this state; and no foreign corporation shall be permitted to transact business within this state unless said foreign corporation is by the laws of the country, state, or territory under which it is formed permitted to transact a like business in such country, state, or territory.

Section 6. Stocks; bonds

No corporation shall issue stock, except to bona fide subscribers therefor or their assignees; nor shall any corporation issue any bond, or other obligation, for the payment of money, except for money or property received or for labor done. The stock of corporations shall not be increased, except in pursuance of a general law, nor shall any law authorize the increase of stock of any corporation without the consent of the person or persons holding the larger amount in value of the stock of such corporation, nor without due notice of the proposed increase having been given as may be prescribed by law. All fictitious increase of stock or indebtedness shall be void.

Section 7. Lease or alienation of franchise

No corporation shall lease or alienate any franchise so as to relieve the franchise, or property held thereunder, from the liabilities of the lessor, or grantor, lessee, or grantee, contracted or incurred in the operation, use, or enjoyment of such franchise or of any of its privileges.

Section 8. Filing of articles of incorporation; place of business; agent for service of process; venue

No domestic or foreign corporation shall do any business in this state without having filed its articles of incorporation or a certified copy thereof with the corporation commission, and without having one or more known places of business and an authorized agent, or agents, in the state upon whom process may be served. Suit may be maintained against a foreign corporation in the county where an agent of such corporation may be found, or in the county where the cause of action may arise.

Section 9. Eminent domain; taking corporate property and franchises for public use

The right of exercising eminent domain shall never be so abridged or construed as to prevent the state from taking the property and the franchises of incorporated companies and subjecting them to public use the same as the property of individuals.

Section 10. Elections for directors or managers

In all elections for directors or managers of any corporation, each shareholder shall have the right to cast as many votes in the aggregate as he shall be entitled to vote in said company under its charter multiplied by the number of directors or managers to be elected at such election; and each shareholder may cast the whole number of votes, either in person or by proxy, for one candidate, or distribute such votes among two or more such candidates; and such directors or managers shall not be elected otherwise.

Section 11. Liability of stockholders

LIABILITY OF STOCKHOLDERS. The shareholders or stockholders of every banking or insurance corporation or association shall be held individually responsible, equally and ratably, and not one for another, for all contracts, debts, and engagements of such corporation or association, to the extent of the amount of their stock therein, at the par value thereof, in addition to the amount invested in such shares or stock; provided, however, that the shareholders or stockholders of any banking corporation or association which is a member of the federal deposit insurance corporation or any successor thereto or other insuring instrumentality of the United States in accordance with the provisions of any applicable law of the United States of America, shall not be liable for any amount in addition to the amount already invested in such shares or stock.

Section 12. Officers of banking institutions; individual responsibility

Any president, director, manager, cashier, or other officer of any banking institution who shall receive, or assent to, the reception of any deposits after he shall have knowledge of the fact that such banking institution is insolvent or in failing circumstances shall be individually responsible for such deposits.

Section 13. Want of legal organization as a defense

No persons acting as a corporation under the laws of Arizona shall be permitted to set up, or rely upon, the want of a legal organization as a defense to any action which may be brought against them as a corporation, nor shall any person or persons who may be sued on a contract now or hereafter made with such corporation, or sued for any injury now or hereafter done to its property, or for a wrong done to its interests, be permitted to rely upon such want of legal organization in his or their defense.

Section 14. Legislative power to impose conditions

This article shall not be construed to deny the right of the legislative power to impose other conditions upon corporations than those herein contained.

15. Monopolies and trusts

Monopolies and trusts shall never be allowed in this state and no incorporated company, co-partnership or association of persons in this state shall directly or indirectly combine or make any contract, with any incorporated company, foreign or domestic, through their stockholders or the trustees or assigns of such stockholders or with any co-partnership or association of persons, or, in any manner whatever, to fix the prices, limit the production, or regulate the transportation of any product or commodity. The legislature shall enact laws for the enforcement of this section by adequate penalties, and in the case of incorporated companies, if necessary for that purpose, may, as a penalty declare a forfeiture of their franchises.

Section 16. Records, books, and files; visitorial and inquisitorial powers of state

The records, books, and files of all public service corporations, state banks, building and loan associations, trust, insurance, and guaranty companies shall be at all times liable and subject to the full visitorial and inquisitorial powers of the state, notwithstanding the immunities and privileges secured in the declaration of rights of this Constitution to persons, inhabitants, and citizens of this state.

Section 17. Fees; reports; licensing of foreign corporations

Provision shall be made by law for the payment of a fee to the state by every domestic corporation, upon the grant, amendment, or extension of its charter, and by every foreign corporation upon its obtaining a license to do business in this state; and also for the payment, by every domestic corporation and foreign corporation doing business in this state, of an annual registration fee of not less than ten dollars, which fee shall be paid irrespective of any specific license or other tax imposed by law upon such company for the privilege of carrying on its business in this state, or upon its franchise or property; and for the making, by every such corporation, at the time of paying such fee, of such report to the corporation commission of the status, business, or condition of such corporation, as may be prescribed by law. No foreign corporation, except insurers, shall have authority to do business in this state, until it shall have obtained from the corporation commission a license to do business in the state, upon such terms as may be prescribed by law. The legislature may relieve any purely charitable, social, fraternal, benevolent, or religious institution from the payment of such annual registration fee.

Section 18. Contributions to influence elections or official action

It shall be unlawful for any corporation, organized or doing business in this state, to make any contribution of money or anything of value for the purpose of influencing any election or official action.

Section 19. Penalties for violation of article

Suitable penalties shall be prescribed by law for the violation of any of the provisions of this article.

Article XV: The Corporation Commission

Section 1. Term limits on corporation commission; composition; election; office vacancies; qualifications

A. No member of the corporation commission shall hold that office for more than two consecutive terms. No corporation commissioner may serve again in that office until out of office for one full term. Any person who serves one half or more of a term shall be considered to have served one term for purposes of this section.

B. A corporation commission is hereby created to be composed of five persons who shall be elected at the general election, and whose term of office shall be four years, and who shall maintain their chief office at the state capital. The two additional commission members shall be elected at the 2002 general election for initial two-year terms beginning on the first Monday in January, 2003. Thereafter, all terms shall be four-year terms.

C. In case of vacancy in the office, the governor shall appoint a commissioner to fill the vacancy. The appointed commissioner shall fill the vacancy until a commissioner shall be elected at a general election as provided by law, and shall qualify. The qualifications of commissioners may be prescribed by law.

Section 2. "Public service corporations" defined

All corporations other than municipal engaged in furnishing gas, oil, or electricity for light, fuel, or power; or in furnishing water for irrigation, fire protection, or other public purposes; or in furnishing, for profit, hot or cold air or steam for heating or cooling purposes; or engaged in collecting, transporting, treating, purifying and disposing of sewage through a system, for profit; or in transmitting messages or furnishing public telegraph or telephone service, and all corporations other than municipal, operating as common carriers, shall be deemed public service corporations.

Section 3. Power of commission as to classifications, rates and charges, rules, contracts, and accounts; local regulation

The corporation commission shall have full power to, and shall, prescribe just and reasonable classifications to be used and just and reasonable rates and charges to be made and collected, by public service corporations within the state for service rendered therein, and make reasonable rules, regulations, and orders, by which such corporations shall be governed in the transaction of business within the state, and may prescribe the forms of contracts and the systems of keeping accounts to be used by such corporations in transacting such business, and make and enforce reasonable rules, regulations, and orders for the convenience, comfort, and safety, and the preservation of the health, of the employees and patrons of such corporations; Provided, that incorporated cities and towns may be authorized by law to exercise supervision over public service corporations doing business therein, including the regulation of rates and charges to be made and collected by such corporations; Provided further, that classifications, rates, charges, rules, regulations, orders, and forms or systems prescribed or made by said corporation commission may from time to time be amended or repealed by such commission.

Section 4. Power to inspect and investigate

The corporation commission, and the several members thereof, shall have power to inspect and investigate the property, books, papers, business, methods, and affairs of any corporation whose stock shall be offered for sale to the public and of any public service corporation doing business within the state, and for the purpose of the commission, and of the several members thereof, shall have the power of a court of general jurisdiction to enforce the attendance of witnesses and the production of evidence by subpoena, attachment, and punishment, which said power shall extend throughout the state. Said commission shall have power to take testimony under commission or deposition either within or without the state.

Section 5. Power to issue certificates of incorporation and licenses

The corporation commission shall have the sole power to issue certificates of incorporation to companies organizing under the laws of this state, and to issue licenses to foreign corporations to do business in this state, except as insurers, as may be prescribed by law.

Domestic and foreign insurers shall be subject to licensing, control and supervision by a department of insurance as prescribed by law. A director of the department of insurance shall be appointed by the governor with the consent of the senate in the manner prescribed by law for a term which may be prescribed by law.

Section 6. Enlargement of powers by legislature; rules and regulations

The law-making power may enlarge the powers and extend the duties of the corporation commission, and may prescribe rules and regulations to govern proceedings instituted by and before it; but, until such rules and regulations are provided by law, the commission may make rules and regulations to govern such proceedings.

Section 7. Connecting and intersecting lines of transportation and communications corporations

Every public service corporation organized or authorized under the laws of the state to do any transportation or transmission business within the state shall have the right to construct and operate lines connecting any points within the state, and to connect at the state boundaries with like lines; and every such corporation shall have the right with any of its lines to cross, intersect, or connect with, any lines of any other public service corporation.

Section 8. Transportation by connecting carriers

Every public service corporation doing a transportation business within the state shall receive and transport, without delay or discrimination, cars loaded or empty, property, or passengers delivered to it by any other public service corporation doing a similar business, and deliver cars, loaded or empty, without delay or discrimination, to other transportation corporations, under such regulations as shall be prescribed by the corporation commission, or by law.

Section 9. Transmission of messages by connecting carriers

Every public service corporation engaged in the business of transmitting messages for profit shall receive and transmit, without delay or discrimination, any messages delivered to it by any other public service corporation engaged in the business of transmitting messages for profit, and shall, with its lines, make physical connection with the lines of any public service corporation engaged in the business of transmitting messages for profit, under such rules and regulations as shall be prescribed by the corporation commission, or by law; Provided, that such public service corporations shall deliver messages to other such corporations, without delay or discrimination, under such rules and regulations as shall be prescribed by the corporation commission, or by law.

Section 10. Railways as public highways; other corporations as common carriers

Railways heretofore constructed, or that may hereafter be constructed, in this state, are hereby declared public highways and all railroads are declared to be common carriers and subject to control by law. All electric, transmission, telegraph, telephone, or pipeline corporations, for the transportation of electricity, messages, water, oil, or other property for profit, are declared to be common carriers and subject to control by law.

Section 11. Movable property as personal property; liability of property to attachment, execution and sale

The rolling stock and all other movable property belonging to any public service corporation in this state, shall be considered personal property, and its real and personal property, and every part thereof, shall be liable to attachment, execution, and sale in the same manner as the property of individuals; and the law-making power shall enact no laws exempting any such property from attachment, execution, or sale.

Section 12. Charges for service; discrimination; free or reduced rate transportation

All charges made for service rendered, or to be rendered, by public service corporations within this state shall be just and reasonable, and no discrimination in charges, service, or facilities shall be made between persons or places for rendering a like and contemporaneous service, except that the granting of free or reduced rate transportation may be authorized by law, or by the corporation commission, to the classes of persons described in the act of Congress approved February 11, 1887, entitled An Act to Regulate Commerce, and the amendments thereto, as those to whom free or reduced rate transportation may be granted.

Section 13. Reports to commission

All public service corporations and corporations whose stock shall be offered for sale to the public shall make such reports to the corporation commission, under oath, and provide such information concerning their acts and operations as may be required by law, or by the corporation commission.

Section 14. Value of property of public service corporations

The corporation commission shall, to aid it in the proper discharge of its duties, ascertain the fair value of the property within the state of every public service corporation doing business therein; and every public service corporation doing business within the state shall furnish to the commission all evidence in its possession, and all assistance in its power, requested by the commission in aid of the determination of the value of the property within the state of such public service corporation.

Section 15. Acceptance of constitutional provisions by existing corporations

No public service corporation in existence at the time of the admission of this state into the union shall have the benefit of any future legislation except on condition of complete acceptance of all provisions of this Constitution applicable to public service corporations.

Section 16. Forfeitures for violations

If any public service corporation shall violate any of the rules, regulations, orders, or decisions of the corporation commission, such corporation shall forfeit and pay to the state not less than one hundred dollars nor more than five thousand dollars for each such violation, to be recovered before any court of competent jurisdiction.

Section 17. Appeal to courts

Nothing herein shall be construed as denying to public service corporations the right of appeal to the courts of the state from the rules, regulations, orders, or decrees fixed by the corporation commission, but the rules, regulations, orders, or decrees so fixed shall remain in force pending the decision of the courts.

Section 19. Power to impose fines

The corporation commission shall have the power and authority to enforce its rules, regulations, and orders by the imposition of such fines as it may deem just, within the limitations prescribed in section 16 of this article.

Article XVI: Militia

Section 1. Composition of militia

The militia of the state of Arizona shall consist of all capable citizens of the state between the ages of eighteen and forty-five years, and of those between said ages who shall have declared their intention to become citizens of the United States, residing therein, subject to such exemptions as now exist, or as may hereafter be created, by the laws of the United States or of this state.

Section 2. Composition and designation of organized militia

The organized militia shall be designated "The National Guard of Arizona," and shall consist of such organized military bodies as now exist under the laws of the territory of Arizona or as may hereafter be authorized by law.

Section 3. Conformity to federal regulations

The organization, equipment, and discipline of the national guard shall conform as nearly as shall be practicable to the regulations for the government of the armies of the United States.

Article XVII: Water Rights

Section 1. Riparian water rights

The common law doctrine of riparian water rights shall not obtain or be of any force or effect in the state.

Section 2. Recognition of existing rights

All existing rights to the use of any of the waters in the state for all useful or beneficial purposes are hereby recognized and confirmed.

Article XVIII: Labor

Section 1. Eight-hour day

Eight hours and no more, shall constitute a lawful day's work in all employment by, or on behalf of, the state or any political subdivision of the State. The legislature shall enact such laws as may be necessary to put this provision into effect, and shall prescribe proper penalties for any violations of said laws.

Section 2. Child labor

No child under the age of fourteen years shall be employed in any gainful occupation at any time during the hours in which the public schools of the district in which the child resides are in session; nor shall any child under sixteen years of age be employed underground in mines, or in any occupation injurious to health or morals or hazardous to life or limb; nor for more than eight hours in any day.

Section 3. Contractual immunity of employer from liability for negligence

It shall be unlawful for any person, company, association, or corporation to require of its servants or employees as a condition of their employment, or otherwise, any contract or agreement whereby such person, company, association, or corporation shall be released or discharged from liability or responsibility on account of personal injuries which may be received by such servants or employees while in the service or employment of such person, company, association, or corporation, by reason of the negligence of such person, company, association, corporation, or the agents or employees thereof; and any such contract or agreement if made, shall be null and void.

Section 4. Fellow servant doctrine

The common law doctrine of fellow servant, so far as it affects the liability of a master for injuries to his servant resulting from the acts or omissions of any other servant or servants of the common master is forever abrogated.

Section 5. Contributory negligence and assumption of risk

The defense of contributory negligence or of assumption of risk shall, in all cases whatsoever, be a question of fact and shall, at all times, be left to the jury.

Section 6. Recovery of damages for injuries

The right of action to recover damages for injuries shall never be abrogated, and the amount recovered shall not be subject to any statutory limitation, except that a crime victim is not subject to a claim for damages by a person who is harmed while the person is attempting to engage in, engaging in or fleeing after having engaged in or attempted to engage in conduct that is classified as a felony offense.

Section 7. Employer's liability law

To protect the safety of employees in all hazardous occupations, in mining, smelting, manufacturing, railroad or street railway transportation, or any other industry the legislature shall enact an employer's liability law, by the terms of which any employer, whether individual, association, or corporation shall be liable for the death or injury, caused by any accident due to a condition or conditions of such occupation, of any employee in the service of such employer in such hazardous occupation, in all cases in which such death or injury of such employee shall not have been caused by the negligence of the employee killed or injured.

Section 8. Workmen's compensation law

The legislature shall enact a workmen's compensation law applicable to workmen engaged in manual or mechanical labor in all public employment whether of the state, or any political subdivision or municipality thereof as may be defined by law and in such private employments as the legislature may prescribe by which compensation shall be required to be paid to any such workman, in case of his injury and to his dependents, as defined by law, in case of his death, by his employer, if in the course of such employment personal injury to or death of any such workman from any accident arising out of and in the course of, such employment, is caused in whole, or in part, or is contributed to, by a necessary risk or danger of such employment, or a necessary risk or danger inherent in the nature thereof, or by failure of such employer, or any of his or its agents or employee or employees to exercise due care, or to comply with any law affecting such employment; provided that it shall be optional with any employee engaged in any such private employment to settle for such compensation, or to retain the right to sue said employer or any person employed by said employer, acting in the scope of his employment, as provided by this Constitution; and, provided further, in order to assure and make certain a just and humane compensation law in the state of Arizona, for the relief and protection of such workmen, their widows, children or dependents, as defined by law, from the burdensome, expensive and litigious remedies for injuries to or death of such workmen, now existing in the state of Arizona, and producing uncertain and unequal compensation therefor, such employee, engaged in such private employment, may exercise the option to settle for compensation by failing to reject the provisions of such workmen's compensation law prior to the injury, except that if the injury is the result of an act done by the employer or a person employed by the employer knowingly and purposely with the direct object of injuring another, and the act indicates a wilful disregard of the life, limb or bodily safety of employees, then such employee may, after the injury, exercise the option to accept compensation or to retain the right to sue the person who injured him.

The percentages and amounts of compensation provided in house bill no. 227 enacted by the seventh legislature of the state of Arizona, shall never be reduced nor any industry included within the provision of said house bill no. 227 eliminated except by initiated or referred measure as provided by this Constitution.

Section 9. Blacklists

The exchange, solicitation, or giving out of any labor "black list," is hereby prohibited, and suitable laws shall be enacted to put this provision into effect.

Section 10. Employment of aliens

No person not a citizen or ward of the United States shall be employed upon or in connection with any state, county or municipal works or employment; provided, that nothing herein shall be construed to prevent the working of prisoners by the state or by any county or municipality thereof on street or road work or other public work and that the provisions of this section shall not apply to the employment of any teacher, instructor, or professor authorized to teach in the United States under the teacher exchange program as provided by federal statutes enacted by the congress of the United States or the employment of university or college faculty members. The legislature shall enact laws for the enforcement and shall provide for the punishment of any violation of this section.

Article XIX: Mines

Section 1. Mines

The office of mine inspector is hereby established. The legislature shall enact laws so regulating the operation and equipment of all mines in the state as to provide for the health and safety of workers therein and in connection therewith, and fixing the duties of said office. Upon approval of such laws by the governor, the governor, with the advice and consent of the senate, shall forthwith appoint a mine inspector, who shall serve until his successor shall have been elected at the first general election thereafter and shall qualify. Said successor and all subsequent incumbents of said office shall be elected at general elections, and shall serve for four years. The initial four year term shall be served by the mine inspector elected in the general election held in November, 1994.

Article XX: Ordinance

The following ordinance shall be irrevocable without the consent of the United States and the people of this state:

First. Toleration of religious sentiment

Perfect toleration of religious sentiment shall be secured to every inhabitant of this state, and no inhabitant of this state shall ever be molested in person or property on account of his or her mode of religious worship, or lack of the same.

Second. Polygamy

Polygamous or plural marriages, or polygamous co-habitation, are forever prohibited within this state.

Third. Introduction of intoxicating liquors into Indian country

The introduction of intoxicating liquors for resale purposes into Indian country is prohibited within this state until July 1, 1957.

Fourth. Public lands; Indian lands

The people inhabiting this state do agree and declare that they forever disclaim all right and title to the unappropriated and ungranted public lands lying within the boundaries thereof and to all lands lying within said boundaries owned or held by any Indian or Indian tribes, the right or title to which shall have been acquired through or from the United States or any prior sovereignty, and that, until the title of such Indian or Indian tribes shall have been extinguished, the same shall be, and remain, subject to the disposition and under the absolute jurisdiction and control of the Congress of the United States.

Fifth. Taxation

The lands and other property belonging to citizens of the United States residing without this state shall never be taxed at a higher rate than the lands and other property situated in this state belonging to residents thereof, and no taxes shall be imposed by this state on any lands or other property within an Indian reservation owned or held by any Indian; but nothing herein shall preclude the state from taxing as other lands and other property are taxed, any lands and other property outside of an Indian reservation owned or held by any Indian, save and except such lands as have been granted or acquired as aforesaid, or as may be granted or confirmed to any Indian or Indians under any act of Congress.

Sixth. Territorial debts and liabilities

The debts and liabilities of the territory of Arizona, and the debts of the counties thereof, valid and subsisting at the time of the passage of the enabling act approved June 20, 1910, are hereby assumed and shall be paid by the state of Arizona, and the state of Arizona shall, as to all such debts and liabilities, be subrogated to all the rights, including rights of indemnity and reimbursement, existing in favor of said territory or of any of the several counties thereof, at the time of the passage of the said enabling act; Provided that nothing in this ordinance shall be construed as validating or in any manner legalizing any territory, county, municipal, or other bonds, obligations, or evidences of indebtedness of said territory or the counties or municipalities thereof which now are or may be invalid or illegal at the time the said state of Arizona is admitted as a state, and the legislature or the people of the state of Arizona shall never pass any law in any manner validating or legalizing the same.

Seventh. Public school system; suffrage

Seventh. Provisions shall be made by law for the establishment and maintenance of a system of public schools which shall be open to all the children of the state and be free from sectarian control, and said schools shall always be conducted in English.

The state shall never enact any law restricting or abridging the right of suffrage on account of race, color, or previous condition of servitude.

Eighth. English language

Eighth. The ability to read, write, speak, and understand the English language sufficiently well to conduct the duties of the office without the aid of an interpreter, shall be a necessary qualification for all state officers and members of the state legislature.

Ninth. Location of state capital

Ninth. The capital of the state of Arizona, until changed by the electors voting at an election provided for by the legislature for that purpose shall be at the city of Phoenix, but no such election shall be called or provided for prior to the thirty-first day of December, nineteen hundred and twenty-five.

Twelfth. Lands granted to state

Twelfth. The state of Arizona and its people hereby consent to all and singular the provisions of the enabling act approved June 20, 1910, concerning the lands thereby granted or confirmed to the state, the terms and conditions upon which said grants and confirmations are made, and the means and manner of enforcing such terms and conditions, all in every respect and particular as in the aforesaid enabling act provided.

Thirteenth. Ordinance as part of constitution; amendment

Thirteenth. This ordinance is hereby made a part of the Constitution of the state of Arizona, and no future constitutional amendment shall be made which in any manner changes or abrogates this ordinance in whole or in part without the consent of Congress.

Article XXI: Mode of Amending

Section 1. Introduction in legislature; initiative petition; election

Any amendment or amendments to this constitution may be proposed in either house of the legislature, or by initiative petition signed by a number of qualified electors equal to fifteen per centum of the total number of votes for all candidates for governor at the last preceding general election. Any proposed amendment or amendments which shall be introduced in either house of the legislature, and which shall be approved by a majority of the members elected to each of the two houses, shall be entered on the journal of each house, together with the ayes and nays thereon. When any proposed amendment or amendments shall be thus passed by a majority of each house of the legislature and entered on the respective journals thereof, or when any elector or electors shall file with the secretary of state any proposed amendment or amendments together with a petition therefor signed by a number of electors equal to fifteen per centum of the total number of votes for all candidates for governor in the last preceding general election, the secretary of state shall submit such proposed amendment or amendments to the vote of the people at the next general election (except when the legislature shall call a special election for the purpose of having said proposed amendment or amendments voted upon, in which case the secretary of state shall submit such proposed amendment or amendments to the qualified electors at said special election,) and if a majority of the qualified electors voting thereon shall approve and ratify such proposed amendment or amendments in said regular or special election, such amendment or amendments shall become a part of this constitution. Until a method of publicity is otherwise provided by law, the secretary of state shall have such proposed amendment or amendments published for a period of at least ninety days previous to the date of said election in at least one newspaper in every county of the state in which a newspaper shall be published, in such manner as may be prescribed by law. If more than one proposed amendment shall be submitted at any election, such proposed amendments shall be submitted in such manner that the electors may vote for or against such proposed amendments separately.

Section 2. Convention

No Convention shall be called by the Legislature to propose alterations, revisions, or amendments to this Constitution, or to propose a new Constitution, unless laws providing for such Convention shall first be approved by the people on a Referendum vote at a regular or special election, and any amendments, alterations, revisions, or new Constitution proposed by such Convention shall be submitted to the electors of the State at a general or special election and be approved by the majority of the electors voting thereon before the same shall become effective.

Article XXII: Schedule and Miscellaneous

Section 1. Existing rights, actions, suits, proceedings, contracts, claims, or demands; process

No rights, actions, suits, proceedings, contracts, claims, or demands, existing at the time of the admission of this State into the Union, shall be affected by a change in the form of government, from Territorial to State, but all shall continue as if no change had taken place; and all process which may have been issued under the authority of the Territory of Arizona, previous to its admission into the Union, shall be as valid as if issued in the name of the State.

Section 2. Territorial laws

All laws of the Territory of Arizona now in force, not repugnant to this Constitution, shall remain in force as laws of the State of Arizona until they expire by their own limitations or are altered or repealed by law; Provided, that wherever the word Territory, meaning the Territory of Arizona, appears in said laws, the word State shall be substituted.

Section 3. Debts, fines, penalties, and forfeitures

All debts, fines, penalties, and forfeitures which have accrued, or may hereafter accrue, to the Territory of Arizona shall inure to the State of Arizona.

Section 4. Recognizances; bonds; estate; judgments; choses in action

All recognizances heretofore taken, or which may be taken, before the change from a Territorial to a State government, shall remain valid, and shall pass to and may be prosecuted in the name of the State, and all bonds executed to the Territory of

Arizona, or to any county or municipal corporation, or to any officer, or court, in his or its official capacity, shall pass to the State authorities and their successors in office for the uses therein expressed, and may be sued for and recovered accordingly; and all the estate, real, personal, and mixed, and all judgments, decrees, bonds, specialties, choses in action, and claims, demands or debts of whatever description, belonging to the Territory of Arizona, shall inure to and vest in the State of Arizona, and may be sued for and recovered by the State of Arizona in the same manner, and to the same extent, as the same might or could have been by the Territory of Arizona.

Section 5. Criminal prosecutions and penal actions; offenses; penalties; actions and suits

All criminal prosecutions and penal actions which may have arisen, or which may arise, before the change from a Territorial to a State government, and which shall then be pending, shall be prosecuted to judgment and execution in the name of the State. All offenses committed against the laws of the Territory of Arizona before the change from a Territorial to a State government, and which shall not be prosecuted before such change, may be prosecuted in the name, and by the authority, of the State of Arizona, with like effect as though such change had not taken place, and all penalties incurred and punishments inflicted shall remain the same as if this Constitution had not been adopted. All actions at law and suits in equity, which may be pending in any of the courts, of the Territory of Arizona at the time of the change from a Territorial to a State government, shall be continued and transferred to the court of the State, or of the United States, having jurisdiction thereof.

Section 6. Territorial, district, county, and precinct officers

All Territorial, district, county, and precinct officers who may be in office at the time of the admission of the State into the Union shall hold their respective offices until their successors shall have qualified, and the official bonds of all such officers shall continue in full force and effect while such officers remain in office.

Section 7. Causes pending in district courts of territory; records, papers, and property

Whenever the judge of the superior court of any county, elected or appointed under the provisions of this Constitution, shall have qualified, the several causes then pending in the district court of the Territory, and in and for such county, except such causes as would have been within the exclusive jurisdiction of the United States courts, had such courts existed at the time of the commencement of such causes within such county, and the records, papers, and proceedings of said district court, and other property pertaining thereto, shall pass into the jurisdiction and possession of the superior court of such county.

It shall be the duty of the clerk of the district court having custody of such papers, records, and property, to transmit to the clerk of said superior court the original papers in all cases pending in such district and belonging to the jurisdiction of said superior court, together with a transcript, or transcripts, of so much of the record of said district court as shall relate to the same; and until the district courts of the Territory shall be superseded in manner aforesaid, and as in this Constitution provided, the said district courts, and the judges thereof, shall continue with the same jurisdiction and powers, to be exercised in the same judicial district, respectively, as heretofore, and now, constituted.

Section 8. Probate records and proceedings

When the State is admitted into the Union, and the superior courts, in their respective counties, are organized, the books, records, papers, and proceedings of the probate court in each county, and all causes and matters of administration pending therein, shall pass into the jurisdiction and possession of the superior court of the same county created by this Constitution, and the said court shall proceed to final judgment or decree, order, or other determination, in the several matters and causes with like effect as the probate court might have done if this Constitution had not been adopted.

Section 9. Causes pending in supreme court of territory; records, papers, and property

Whenever a quorum of the judges of the Supreme Court of the State shall have been elected, and qualified, and shall have taken office, under this Constitution, the causes then pending in the Supreme Court of the Territory, except such causes as would have been within the exclusive jurisdiction of the United States courts, had such courts existed at the time of the commencement of such causes, and the papers, records, and proceedings of said court, and the seal and other property pertaining thereto, shall pass into the jurisdiction and possession of the Supreme Court of the State, and until so superseded, the Supreme Court of the Territory, and the judges thereof, shall continue, with like powers and jurisdiction as if this Constitution had not been adopted, or the State admitted into the Union; and all causes pending in the Supreme Court of the Territory at said time, and which said causes would have been within the exclusive jurisdiction of the United States courts, had such courts existed, at the time of the commencement of such causes, and the papers, records, and proceedings of said court, relating thereto, shall pass into the jurisdiction of the United States courts, all as in the Enabling Act approved June 20, 1910, provided.

Section 10. Seals of supreme court, superior courts, municipalities, and county officers

Until otherwise provided by law, the seal now in use in the Supreme Court of the Territory, shall be the seal of the Supreme Court of the State, except that the word "State", shall be substituted for the word "Territory" on said seal. The seal of the superior courts of the several counties of the State, until otherwise provided by law, shall be the vignette of Abraham Lincoln, with the words "Seal of the Superior Court of _____ County, State of Arizona, surrounding the vignette. The seal of municipalities, and of all county officers, in the Territory, shall be the seals of such municipalities and county officers, respectively, under the State, until otherwise provided by law, except that the word "Territory", or "Territory of Arizona", be changed to read "State" or "State of Arizona", where the same may appear on any such seals.

Section 11. Effective date of constitution

The provisions of this Constitution shall be in force from the day on which the President of the United States shall issue his proclamation declaring the State of Arizona admitted into the Union.

Section 12. Election of representative in congress

One Representative in the Congress of the United States shall be elected from the State at large, and at the same election at which officers shall be elected under the Enabling Act, approved June 20, 1910, and, thereafter, at such times and in such manner as may be prescribed by law.

Section 13. Continuation in office until qualification of successor

The term of office of every officer to be elected or appointed under this Constitution or the laws of Arizona shall extend until his successor shall be elected and shall qualify.

Section 14. Initiative

Any law which may be enacted by the Legislature under this Constitution may be enacted by the people under the Initiative. Any law which may not be enacted by the Legislature under this Constitution shall not be enacted by the people.

Section 15. Public institutions

Correctional and penal institutions, and institutions for the benefit of persons who have mental or physical disabilities and such other institutions as the public good may require, shall be established and supported by the State in such manner as may be prescribed by law.

Section 16. Confinement of minor offenders

It shall be unlawful to confine any minor under the age of eighteen years, accused or convicted of crime, in the same section of any jail or prison in which adult prisoners are confined. Suitable quarters shall be prepared for the confinement of such minors.

Section 17. Compensation of public officers

All State and county officers (except notaries public) and all justices of the peace and constables, whose precinct includes a city or town or part thereof, shall be paid fixed and definite salaries, and they shall receive no fees for their own use.

Section 19. Lobbying

The Legislature shall enact laws and adopt rules prohibiting the practice of lobbying on the floor of either House of the Legislature, and further regulating the practice of lobbying.

Section 20. Design of state seal

The seal of the State shall be of the following design: In the background shall be a range of mountains, with the sun rising behind the peaks thereof, and at the right side of the range of mountains there shall be a storage reservoir and a dam, below which in the middle distance are irrigated fields and orchards reaching into the foreground, at the right of which are cattle grazing. To the left in the middle distance on a mountain side is a quartz mill in front of which and in the foreground is a miner standing with pick and shovel. Above this device shall be the motto: "Ditat Deus." In a circular band surrounding the whole device shall be inscribed: "Great Seal of The State of Arizona", with the year of admission of the State into the Union.

Section 21. Enactment of laws to carry constitution into effect

The Legislature shall enact all necessary laws to carry into effect the provisions of this Constitution.

Section 22. Judgments of death

The judgment of death shall be inflicted by administering an intravenous injection of a substance or substances in a lethal quantity sufficient to cause death except that defendants sentenced to death for offenses committed prior to the effective date of the amendment to this section shall have the choice of either lethal injection or lethal gas. The lethal injection or lethal gas shall be administered under such procedures and supervision as prescribed by law. The execution shall take place within the limits of the state prison.

Article XXV: Right to Work

Section 1. Right to work or employment without membership in labor organization

No person shall be denied the opportunity to obtain or retain employment because of non-membership in a labor organization, nor shall the State or any subdivision thereof, or any corporation, individual or association of any kind enter into any agreement, written or oral, which excludes any person from employment or continuation of employment because of non-membership in a labor organization.

Article XXVI: Right of Licensed Real Estate Brokers and Salesmen to Prepare Instruments Incident to Property Transactions

Section 1. Powers of real estate broker or salesman

Any person holding a valid license as a real estate broker or a real estate salesman regularly issued by the Arizona State Real Estate Department when acting in such capacity as broker or salesman for the parties, or agent for one of the parties to a sale, exchange, or trade, or the renting and leasing of property, shall have the right to draft or fill out and complete, without charge, any and all instruments incident thereto including, but not limited to, preliminary purchase agreements and earnest money receipts, deeds, mortgages, leases, assignments, releases, contracts for sale of realty, and bills of sale.

Article XXVII: Regulation of Health, Safety, and Welfare

Section 1. Regulation of ambulances; powers of legislature

The legislature may provide for the regulation of ambulances and ambulance services in this state in all matters relating to services provided, routes served, response times and charges.

Article XXVIII: English as the Official Language

Section 1. Definitions

In this article, unless the context otherwise requires:

1. "Government" includes all laws, public proceedings, rules, publications, orders, actions, programs, policies, departments, boards, agencies, organizations and instrumentalities of this state or political subdivisions of this state, as appropriate under the circumstances to a particular official action.

2. "Official action" includes the performance of any function or action on behalf of this state or a political subdivision of this state or required by state law that appears to present the views, position or imprimatur of the state or political subdivision or that binds or commits the state or political subdivision, but does not include:

(a) The teaching of or the encouragement of learning languages other than English.

(b) Actions required under the federal individuals with disabilities education act or other federal laws.

(c) Actions, documents or policies necessary for tourism, commerce or international trade.

(d) Actions or documents that protect the public health and safety, including law enforcement and emergency services.

(e) Actions that protect the rights of victims of crimes or criminal defendants.

(f) Using terms of art or phrases from languages other than English.

(g) Using or preserving Native American languages.

(h) Providing assistance to hearing impaired or illiterate persons.

(i) Informal and nonbinding translations or communications among or between representatives of government and other persons if this activity does not affect or impair supervision, management, conduct or execution of official actions and if the representatives of government make clear that these translations or communications are unofficial and are not binding on this state or a political subdivision of this state.

(j) Actions necessary to preserve the right to petition for the redress of grievances.

3. "Preserve, protect and enhance the role of English" includes:

(a) Avoiding any official actions that ignore, harm or diminish the role of English as the language of government.

(b) Protecting the rights of persons in this state who use English.

(c) Encouraging greater opportunities for individuals to learn the English language.

(d) To the greatest extent possible under federal statute, providing services, programs, publications, documents and materials in English.

4. "Representatives of government" includes all individuals or entities during the performance of the individual's or entity's official actions.

Section 2. Official language of Arizona

The official language of the state of Arizona is English.

Section 3. Preserving and enhancing the role of the official
language; right to use English

A. Representatives of government in this state shall preserve, protect and enhance the role of English as the official language of the government of Arizona.

B. A person shall not be discriminated against or penalized in any way because the person uses or attempts to use English in public or private communication.

Section 4. Official actions to be conducted in English

Official actions shall be conducted in English.

Section 5. Rules of construction

This article shall not be construed to prohibit any representative of government, including a member of the legislature, while performing official duties, from communicating unofficially through any medium with another person in a language other than English if official action is conducted in English.

Section 6. Standing; notification of attorney general; recovery of costs

A. A person who resides or does business in this state may file a civil action for relief from any official action that violates this article in a manner that causes injury to the person.

B. A person who resides or does business in this state and who contends that this article is not being implemented or enforced may file a civil action to determine if the failure or inaction complained of is a violation of this article and for injunctive or mandatory relief.

C. A person shall not file an action under this section unless the person has notified the attorney general of the alleged violation and the attorney general or other appropriate representative of government has not provided appropriate relief within a reasonable time under the circumstances. An action filed under this section may be in addition to or in lieu of any action by officers of this state, including the attorney general.

D. A person who files and is successful in an action under this section may be awarded all costs expended or incurred in the action, including reasonable attorney fees.

Article XXIX: Public Retirement Systems

Section 1. Public retirement systems

A. Public retirement systems shall be funded with contributions and investment earnings using actuarial methods and assumptions that are consistent with generally accepted actuarial standards.

B. The assets of public retirement systems, including investment earnings and contributions, are separate and independent trust funds and shall be invested, administered and distributed as determined by law solely in the interests of the members and beneficiaries of the public retirement systems.

C. Membership in a public retirement system is a contractual relationship that is subject to article II, section 25.

D. Public retirement system benefits shall not be diminished or impaired, except that certain adjustments to the public safety personnel retirement system may be made as provided in senate bill 1428, as enacted by the fifty-second legislature, second regular session.

E. This section preserves the authority vested in the legislature pursuant to this constitution and does not restrict the legislature's ability to modify public retirement system benefits for prospective members of public retirement systems.

Article XXX: Marriage

Section 1. Marriage

Only a union of one man and one woman shall be valid or recognized as a marriage in this state.

www.ingramcontent.com/pod-product-compliance
Lightning Source LLC
Chambersburg PA
CBHW052254220526
45471CB00001B/335